MW00479518

The Things We Do for Love

Ruhama Veltfort was a young Barnard graduate living on the Lower East Side of Manhattan when she gave up her newborn son for adoption. Thirty-one years later, she discovered that he was living only five blocks away from her home in San Francisco's Mission District.

With tenderness and wry humor, these fourteen well-observed stories trace the roots of that cycle of relinquishment and reunion, offering an intimate perspective on the social transformations of the mid-to-late twentieth century. Lovers, husbands, children and a "rag-tag band of seekers and screwballs" wind their way through this vivid and even-handed memoir of a Bohemian "red-diaper" childhood in 1950's California, a rebellious coming-of-age in the earliest days of the Grateful Dead and an Ivy League education gone sour. Universal themes of idealism, betrayal and redemption weave through a moving account of the author's adventures in political activism and the human potential movement to culminate in a maturity graced by family, friends and an eclectic spirituality.

Also by Ruhama Veltfort

The Promised Land

"Other writers have related the brave stories of Jewish immigrant pioneers who made their way from tiny villages in Eastern Europe to the vast open spaces and new possibilities of the American West, but Ruhama Veltfort, in her impressive first novel, recasts the tale in a spiritual dimension."

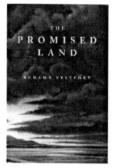

— Sandee Brawarsky,
The New York Times Book Review

"This is a rich and rewarding novel, a tapestry of many closely interwoven themes, including religious identity, faith and doubt, tradition and innovation, exile and return. It's a poignant portrait of an extraordinary marriage."

— Merle Rubin, *The Christian Science Monitor*

"... Veltfort has gone beyond following tradition here and instead has created what many in the book business have hoped for but thought impossible: a novel true to both literary and spiritual traditions."

— Mardi Link, *ForeWord*

The Things We Do for Love

Stories of My Life

———————————————

Ruhama Veltfort

THE THINGS WE DO FOR LOVE
© 2010 by Ruhama Veltfort

ISBN 978-1-931002-89-9

Book design by Jo-Anne Rosen

Cover image: "The Fall" by Lucas Cranach the Elder
Used by permission of Art Resource (www.artres.com)

Wordrunner Press
Petaluma, California
www.wordrunner.com/publish

Contents

The Things We Do for Love

Steel Tents

It's summer, and we are going to Steel Tents. It's a house on a beach on Cape Ann, Massachusetts, where Nanny stays in the summer. She doesn't like to be called "Grandma" like other kids call their grandmothers: she has to be Nanny, like a goat. She doesn't have white hair or bake cookies like a real grandmother, either. She's very small, and she has shiny reddish-brown hair, and she has a name like no one else in the world: Tola.

Nanny and my mother come from Europe. They used to live in Paris, but my mother was born in Vienna, and Nanny came from Poland. People say my mother's accent is cute, but you can hardly understand what Nanny says at all. She doesn't always understand what I say, either, and she leans into me, all smelly and twinkly, a huge gap between her front teeth, and asks: *"Vot?"* It's embarrassing, her hot stinky breath pushing out in front of her French perfume, and I lean away. She pulls me close against her cheek, slack as an empty balloon. *"Mooshki,"* she coos. That's Polish for "little mouse."

Daddy takes us to San Francisco, to the airport, and my mother and my baby sister and I fly to Boston. I sit by the window so I can watch the propellers. Sometimes fire comes out behind them, but my mother says it's all right, it always does that. She says when she was a little girl she and Nanny used to fly in a little tiny airplane over the Alps! Our voices buzz when we talk. The

1

stewardess gives me a metal junior stewardess pin with wings on it, but Annie is just a baby so she doesn't get one. When we get our dinner everything rattles on the little tray.

Nanny picks us up at the airport in her little round car that looks like a black sow bug. It's a convertible, but she doesn't put the top down. Her house is almost as big as a castle, with three stories and five bathrooms. There's a hidden staircase too, and lots and lots of closets, some as big as little rooms. It's hard to fall asleep in the big bed with crisp, ironed sheets. The room I'm in is filled with dark furniture and strange things. There's a leather-framed photograph of my child-mother with my young grandparents in their Paris lives. Nanny looks like a movie star in an old movie; my famous dead grandfather has a round face and big black eyeglasses. Between them is my mother, a little girl with a dark Buster Brown haircut, in white stockings and a dress with a short, flared skirt.

From Sparks Street half a block away I hear the steady swish of traffic. The loud, buzzing hum is Nanny's air conditioner, in her bedroom across the hall. Even the air outside here feels foreign: hot and spongy. They call it "muggy" — I used to think that was one of my father's made-up words, because he always makes a face when he says it.

Nanny has a big black poodle named Romy. His real name is Romulus, and his littermate, Remus, belonged to Tante Deidre, Nanny's friend. I know the story about the real Romulus and Remus. My mother told me my grandfather, Otto Rank — another funny name — wrote a book about stories of lost children who were saved in strange ways. On a desk in my room here is a small bronze copy of a famous sculpture of the babies suckling from the she-wolf's dangly teats. It's disgusting and embarrassing; I hate to look at it.

Romy the dog is embarrassing, too — he's a face-licker and crotch sniffer. He isn't very friendly — he only loves Nanny. She says he's jealous of me, the way she says I'm jealous of my baby sister. Romy is so jealous of anyone Nanny pays attention to that he's gouged deep scratches in the soundproof door to the special room downstairs where Nanny sees her patients. Her patients are called *analysands* — a word with a hiss in it that makes me think of the beach.

After we stay in muggy Cambridge for two days, we drive to Cape Ann. I'm glad Romy is staying with Tante Deirdre. Nanny drives the round, black car. She doesn't want my mother to drive, even though she's so short she has to prop herself up with pillows. Even then she can barely see over the hood with the shiny Indian chief ornament. She hunches over the wheel, squinting like The Nearsighted Mr. Magoo. My mother keeps going *whsst*, drawing in air through her teeth, every time she thinks we're going to crash.

We're going to Gloucester, to the Ames Estate, where some other families — Nanny's friends — rent summer houses. Nanny stays in a big house, but we have a small cottage made out of metal, named Steel Tents. It's painted a bright pink that all the grownups make fun of, but I secretly think it's beautiful. Every couple of days it rains, and my mother complains about the deafening, rattling noise of the rain falling on the metal roof. The din excites me almost to the point of terror. My father likes to read me scary fairy tales about huts in the forest where heroes and witches sleep, and, especially in the rain, the dark interior of Steel Tents, smelling of musty dampness, makes me feel like I'm in one of those stories.

Back home in Palo Alto, it never rains in the summertime. The trees look and smell different, and the bright and sparkly ocean here is a different ocean. The waves here sometimes come as high as my chest, but they are not the giant towering rollers of the beach at home, that suck the sand out from around your feet when they draw back. I can wade out into the water here — all the way up to my neck if I want.

Every day or so we make an excursion through the bright green-leafed streets of Gloucester to the white clapboard post office, to the grocery store, to the slippery, smelly fishing docks to buy lobsters. All the grownups love lobsters, but I hate them — ugly monsters with scary pincers. They hiss and turn from their dark bottom-of-the-sea green to bright red as the cook drops them, wriggling, into boiling water. At dinner, draped in napkins like babies — bibs I am too grown-up myself to wear — Nanny and my mother and Nanny's friends, the DeVotos and the Rochlins crack their giant potato bugs open with nutcrackers and pick at them with little pointed tools, smacking their lips. Mark DeVoto is the only one of the children to eat lobster. The Rochlin kids and I dip Parker House rolls in the melted butter and eat hamburgers and hot dogs, making faces at each other.

This summer I am just on the cusp of real childhood, and Mark, a few years older, is my initiator into the rituals of that world. He is wild and loud and clever, even more precocious than I am. Wiry and dark, tanned — like an Indian, Nanny says — he defies the all-powerful grownups and climbs trees to the highest branches.

Avis, his mother, stands looking up with her hands on her hips and her sharp elbows sticking out, shouting, "Come down from there this instant!"

Mark's father Benny, watching from a big green wooden chair on the porch, puffs on his cigarette. "Huck Finn," he winks knowingly at my grandmother, sitting beside him.

"Ah, Huck!" Nanny nods wisely, smiling up at Benny.

Mark swings crazily high on the tire that hangs from a tree by a rope, and leaps off onto the grass. He goes in the water right after lunch, instead of waiting an hour like you're supposed to. He is too old to take a nap. He won't put on a sweater when the wind turns chilly in the evening. He teaches me card games: War, Go Fish, I Doubt It. In his pocket, he carries a little notebook where he's made a list of insults and nasty names to call people. I admire him, I adore him, I run after him everywhere.

His father is Nanny's special friend. Her face softens when she says his name: Benny. In the sunset evenings they sit together on the porch of the big house, screened safe from mosquitoes, drinking scotch poured from bottles with little black and white dogs or sailing ships on the labels. Benny leans forward to light Nanny's Parliament cigarette in its tortoise-shell holder. Nanny bends her head towards him; her eyes seem to grow bigger, her red-lipstick mouth makes a funny little smile, her lips kept closed. "Tola," he murmurs. Avis swirls her drink around in her glass, making the ice cubes jangle, and smashes out her own red-smeared cigarette in the black onyx ashtray, even though it's only half smoked.

Mark tells me his father is very famous. I think he is probably more famous than my famous dead grandfather who no one I know has ever heard of. Mark's father has written lots of books, and he writes a column every two weeks for an important magazine. That's what he is busy doing every afternoon, when the rest of us are at the beach. To me, Mark's famous father is only slightly more intimidating than the other baffling grownups, large, coarse creatures who do not like to get wet or sandy at the beach, who talk louder and faster as they drink their glasses of golden-colored scotch, whose laughter is frightening, not funny at all.

The Ames Estate has its own beach, a scallop of sand with rocks at one end to climb on. Soft little waves curl against the shore. The sand is rough and warm. I have a two-piece bathing suit, ruffled, light blue printed with tiny pink and white lambs. I insist on wearing the top, even though my mother says I don't need it. I hate it when she laughs at me. My mother laughs, and Nanny talks to her in French: "*Chérie*," she says, and then "*bla bla bla.*" They always talk in French when they don't want me to understand them.

But it's my bathing suit, and it has two pieces, and I will wear both of them, not just the bottom, like a boy. I run back and forth between the waves and the sand. I run over the hot sand into the cold, bright wave water, into the water, up to my waist, my chest. Chilly, I run out, out of the water, over the wet sand, into the dry sand, toward the blankets where the grownups lie.

Nanny and my mother read books in French, slitting the pages with a little dagger that lies between them on their blanket. It's too early for the scotch bottles, with their little dogs and sailing ships; instead, there are shiny cans of beer propped in the sand. The grownups all wear dark glasses, hiding their eyes. They smell of Skol, sun tan oil in brown bottles. Nanny wears a blue and white bathing suit with a skirt. Below it, her pale white legs are crisscrossed with tiny purple veins. "The best legs in Paris!" she's boasted to me, lifting her skirt. When she was twenty, she says, she won a contest.

Mark's mother Avis lies on her blanket. Her body is long and thin and dark, in her black bathing suit. Her sharp nose is coated with white cream below her sunglasses. Her red lipstick smears the end of her cigarette when she sucks on it. I run into the water, I run out of the water. I run past the blankets where the grownups lie. Sand spins up beneath my feet.

"Stop that! Don't kick sand!" Avis yells at me.

I run back into the waves, up to my waist, up to my chest, up to my neck. I'm alone in the water. Mark is off somewhere, probably climbing a tree. He is an only child. There was a baby that died; my mother told me, then told me not to talk about it. The Rochlin kids and their parents went out sailing today.

I run out of the water, through the sand, past the blankets. Avis sits up, stands up. She grabs me by the arm and her free hand lands on my behind, hard — once, twice, three times.

I'm stunned and enraged. My parents spank me, but not often. What have I done? I didn't kick sand, the sand flew up from my feet! My feet fly back, I run back into the water. I don't cry. I run back into the water, up to my knees, my waist — and then a howl escapes, a wild wail from deep in my chest. My mother is suddenly beside me, carrying me out of the water. My tears splash hot as I struggle against her.

"A wave must have knocked her down," I hear her say, carrying me past the grownups on their blankets, carrying me back to Steel Tents.

I try to remember the insults and nasty names from Mark's notebook. *Dippy, dopey, double-disconnected, doggone dim-witted dumbbell.* I think now I understand him a little better. *I'm rubber and you're glue,* I think. *Everything you say bounces off me and sticks to you!*

My mother says she's sorry, Avis shouldn't have spanked me, but I should be more careful about not kicking sand. I shake my head. "I don't care," I say. "I was just crying because a wave knocked me down." My mother goes back out to the beach. I'm shivering. I wrap myself up in a towel. I won't come out until supper time.

That night when Nanny tucks me in, I whisper in her ear: "I was crying because Avis spanked me." I whisper, so only Nanny will know.

"*Vot?*" The vapor of her breath, heavy with golden scotch, escapes from the gap between her teeth. When she presses against me I smell her perfume. Smelling it, I can see the little carved glass bottle in the brown box. *Mitsouko,* it's called. The sweet, strong perfume of the glamorous woman in the photo, with dark hair pressed close around her face like a slick helmet. Her lips closed over the front-tooth gap, curved in a Mona Lisa smile. The most beautiful legs in Paris.

"Mooshki," she croons. Her fingers reach for my cheek and pinch it, like a lobster.

Rescuing Annie

My sister and I were too young to go on the plane by ourselves, so my mother's cousin Sascha flew with us. I was eight and Annie five. Sascha was in college at Berkeley, and was flying to Boston to see his family. Annie and I were going to visit Nanny, by ourselves.

I was so excited that I threw up on the plane and some got on Annie's coat. She was mad, but I told her it paid her back for the time when she was a baby and pooped in the bathtub when we were taking a bath together. But we didn't fight too much because we liked Sascha and we were trying to act grown-up. We had never been on a trip without our parents before, but they said they needed to have a long talk by themselves and so they sent us to Nanny's.

I loved Nanny's house. I loved the cream puffs that Catherine made especially for me, and the Dutch chocolate shaped like an apple that broke apart in sections, and the Sachertorte from the Window Shop. The pillows on the bed were the softest, the sheets the crispest. It was hard to understand what Nanny said, and she hugged too hard, and kissed too wetly — but she bought me anything I wanted and never yelled at me. Her "young doctors" came to visit every day; they and their pretty wives took us to the Science Museum and to the Swan Boats and told Nanny how smart and pretty we were. The young doctors were Nanny's patients; they were learning how to be psychoanalysts.

Annie didn't like it at Nanny's as much as I did. She missed Mommy, and she got asthma and she whined. Whatever I said I wanted, she wanted the exact same thing, and Nanny teased her about copying me and made her cry. But Annie liked the chocolates and pastries as much as I did, and she liked all the bathrooms in Nanny's house — five, counting the little one in back of the kitchen and the one in the attic apartment that nobody lived in.

We had our own bathroom, in the upstairs hall near the big room we slept in. We usually took baths in Nanny's bathroom, but one evening after dinner Annie wanted to take a bath in our own bathroom, and somehow, while the tub was filling, she went in to use the toilet and locked herself in.

Annie rattled at the door. In the background, the water was running. She yelled for help. I tried to explain to her how to turn the metal catch just below the doorknob, but she was too scared to listen. While Nanny shouted encouragements, Elizabeth, the maid, poked a hairpin ineffectually into the keyhole. Nanny yelled at Elizabeth. Annie cried.

"See the metal thing, Annie?" I cajoled. "Turn the metal thing, push on it."

"I *count!*" Annie wailed. Her pronunciation drove me wild — her version of our mother's Viennese/Boston vowels.

"*Can't! Can't!*" I screamed.

"*I count!*"

"I am calling Doctor Farber," Nanny shouted. He was one of her young men.

He came with his friend, Dr. Wilbur. They consulted at the door. Dr. Farber was tall and thin, with black hair, and Dr. Wilbur was much shorter, and had blond curly hair and thick glasses. The water thundered, Annie howled. Nanny seemed to think Annie would drown if the door wasn't opened, or the water turned off.

"Maybe she can turn the water off," suggested Dr. Farber. He tapped nervously at the door. "Annie? Hello, Annie, this is Bill Farber — remember the Swan Boats? Can you turn off the faucet, Annie?"

"Annie," I said. "Stop crying and listen!"

"*I count!*" she cried.

Dr. Wilbur put his shoulder to the door and shoved. The door didn't move. He stood back. "Bill, maybe if we both take a run at it — "

The two of them stepped back into the hall, about five feet from the door. Nanny grabbed me and squished as I wriggled. I could feel how frightened she was.

"One ... Two ... THREE!" The two men ran at the door, hitting it with an enormous thud. The door rattled, but did not move. Annie screamed. Dr. Wilbur rubbed his shoulder.

"Do you have an axe, Tola?" he asked. "Maybe we should just break the door in."

"I'll check the woodpile." Dr. Farber ran downstairs.

Annie was sniffling and hiccupping behind the door.

"Just try to turn the faucet off, Annie," I counseled. I was beginning to worry.

"But I count," she whined. "The water's running."

Dr. Farber came running up the stairs with a hatchet and warned me to stand back. I cowered in Nanny's arms. He swung the axe and struck the door. Annie screamed, "The door is breaking!"

I started to cry.

"Stop, stop!" Nanny was angry. "You are frightening the children!"

"Maybe you should call the fire department, Tola." Dr. Wilbur suggested.

Nanny ran downstairs to the phone. They came very quickly, three big men in yellow slickers and red hats. It was like something in a book. After they came in and looked at the door, they left.

"Where are they going?" I asked.

"Shh," Nanny said. "Don't worry, darling. I'll protect you. You and your little sister are safe."

"They're going to go in through the window," Dr. Wilbur said, with satisfaction.

"Annie," I ran up to the bathroom door. "Annie, the fireman is going to come through the window and rescue you!" I wondered if she was going to get to jump into a net.

In a minute the water stopped. One of the firemen had squeezed through the tiny bathroom window and shut off the tap. He opened the door and Annie rushed out. Her face was red and streaked.

"I want Mommy," she sobbed.

Nanny hugged her. "Mommy is in California! Nanny is here! Nanny called the firemen to save you! Come downstairs, Catherine is still here, she will make you chocolate." She offered Dr. Wilbur and Dr. Farber a scotch, but they said goodnight and went home.

We went down to the kitchen. Catherine and Elizabeth were sitting at the table. Elizabeth had her coat on. Her white starchy apron was hanging behind the door. Catherine was big and had brown skin and wore a green uniform dress, but Elizabeth was small and white, with gray hair and a freckled face. She stood up when my grandmother came into the kitchen. She picked up her black purse. "Well goodnight, Dr. R.," she said. "I'm going now. We can thank the good Lord for the boys from the Fire Department."

Catherine usually went home as soon as she finished washing the dinner dishes, but she had stayed because of the commotion.

She made us hot chocolate with a marshmallow in it. Nanny poured scotch from the bottle with the sailing ship on it into a Welch's grape jelly glass. She lifted her drink to us. "*A santé*," she said fondly. "Beautiful children."

Trini

My father had a maroon Ford convertible, a '49, and he liked to go for rides in the country on Sundays. He liked to drive into the hills behind Palo Alto: Alpine Road, Skyline, La Honda — this was years before the freeways were built, before those roads became cluttered with fancy houses. The hills were still wild then, soft with gold grass, spotted with orange poppies and blue lupine and the big live-oaks that stretched their arms out into the sky. Daddy drove with the top down and when a girlfriend rode in front with him Annie and I bounced in the back seat.

The girlfriends complained that he drove too fast around those curves, and the wind whipped my hair hard against my face, stinging like little knives. I squinched my face up with suffering and waited for Daddy to stop the car to look at the view, so I could look through a curl of my hair and see it sparkle golden brown in the sun against that blue sky that went on and on. Annie pressed up close against me, and I tried to wiggle away. I couldn't bear to be touched by her; I could hardly bear to be touched by anyone. I was a lone child, a reader and a brooder, and I slipped easily in and out of the world of magic, where cats talked and fairies whispered. I resented grownups and other children alike for their relentless need to keep me engaged in their flat, hard country.

My father was a handsome man, tall and slim, with clear, light blue eyes and curly brown hair. I was angry at my mother for sending him away; I knew it was all her fault. My father was an engineer, but after the divorce he'd quit his engineer job and was working in a paint factory. He worked the graveyard shift, which sounded scary and interesting to me, but when he drove by the factory one day to show it to us, it was just a big gray building. I didn't see any tombstones. I felt stupid, like when I was Annie's age and thought his job had something to do with trains.

After the divorce we all moved. Mother and Annie and I moved to the house on Windermere. First Daddy lived in a room over the Shapovalovs' garage, and then he moved to the place on Loma Verde Avenue in South Palo Alto. Loma Verde was nearly in the country then, a road that tapered off into dirt, with only a few houses scattered along it. Just before Daddy moved I overheard him telling the Shapovalovs about his new house. I was always eavesdropping — I was only eight, and no one would tell me anything interesting. Daddy said his new place had a big workshop in front and "living quarters" in back, and I didn't understand what he meant. I had been reading by myself since I was four and I knew a lot of words, but I had never heard of "living quarters" — only "hindquarters" and "headquarters." I wanted to see those "living quarters."

Daddy's new house was a low, shabby bungalow, set back from the street, with a broad patch of dirt at the end of the driveway. A few wooden steps led up to a wide, shallow room with an old green couch in it. Beyond this room, on the left, was the workshop, smelling of solder, like Daddy smelled. There were long work tables on sawhorses, covered with the mysterious tiny pieces of metal and colored wire that he used to build radios and things. There were the instruments he used: the oscilloscope with the green line of light making wavy designs across the small round screen; the tube tester with its red, yellow and green lights; the dangerous, red-hot soldering iron. Trays and little plastic boxes were crammed with tiny things that Daddy tried to teach me the names of, but I could never tell the resistors from the capacitators, and some pieces had names I couldn't remember at all.

What Daddy meant by "living quarters" was his bedroom, with lots of bookshelves and his wide, low bed covered with an olive-drab Army blanket. Behind the bedroom was a big kitchen with the lonely table and chairs, and behind that, a toilet and a shower. He didn't have a bathtub. When Annie and I spent the night, we slept in the funny long room at the very front of the house that was like a closed-in front porch. Daddy put the cushions from the couch on the floor and made little beds for us there. He was proud of his new home, but it seemed odd to me, as if it wasn't quite finished.

I worried about him. For his birthday, I bought him a set of dishes at the five-and-ten, milky green glass plates, bowls, cups, and saucers: four of each. The big plates cost twenty-five cents each, and the other pieces a little less. They made a big package, all those dishes, and the whole set cost five or six dollars, but I didn't care. I had money that Nanny sent me for birthdays and Christmas, and I made my mother let me take it out of the bank, because Daddy needed proper dishes.

I missed our old two-story house with the palm trees in front and the cherry-plum tree in the side yard outside my window. My mother was often angry — or "impatient," as she called it. She expected me to help her by doing chores around the house and taking care of Annie, and I didn't like to. Sometimes with no warning she got very angry at me for no reason at all. But even though I missed Daddy, visiting him made me nervous in some way that I didn't understand. Annie was only four, a silly baby, and when we were at Daddy's she cried and wanted Mommy, and sometimes she got asthma.

Daddy sometimes tried to cheer us up when we were there, but most of the time he worked in his workshop. He lifted us up onto tall stools to watch him, but it was very boring, and after a few minutes I wanted to get down and read or draw. And then Annie would want to get down too, and Daddy would tell me I had to play with her, and she would pester me so I couldn't even read.

One day I was complaining. When he'd lived at the Shapovalovs, Mrs. Shapovalov used to bake cookies for us, so Daddy said he would bake us a cake. He bought a box of spice cake mix and baked it a little too long in a loaf pan, and then he wouldn't put icing on it because he said icing was silly and we didn't need it. It was an awful cake. It wasn't at all what I had been thinking of — a high, white, fluffy cake with chocolate icing, like in a magazine picture. I didn't want to hurt his feelings — hurt feelings, I understood, had been the cause of the divorce — but I didn't like that spice cake. I only ate a little.

Daddy had lots of different girlfriends, and some I liked better than others. Now there was Trini. She was very pretty, with long, curly, black hair, and she wore glasses, like my mother — in fact, she looked a little like my mother. But my mother yelled, and Trini was nice; she was gentle and tentative where my mother was impetuous and forceful. I think she seemed younger than my parents and the other grownups I knew. I was especially happy that she didn't have any children — most of Daddy's girlfriends did, and I had to play with them whether I liked them or not.

I figured out Trini was Daddy's girlfriend one afternoon when he picked us up to stay with him for the weekend. Annie and I sat in the front seat with him. "Do you like Trini?" he asked. "How would you like it if we got married?" I was excited and amazed, but

I was also wary, because I knew that sometimes when grownups asked if you wanted something and you said yes, you still didn't get it. I had even begun to think that saying you wanted something might somehow keep it away. Daddy was happy, singing as he drove, before he asked us that.

I loved Trini. I wanted her to be my mother, with her long black curly hair, her wide mouth. She laughed and sparkled. She was an artist, and I understood art to be a kind of magic. She gave me a watercolor picture she'd painted of a chair in shades of green, all curves and angles. It looked like the chair had been broken into pieces and then put back together a little differently. Trini mounted it on a black mat and I put it on the wall of my room at home. My mother said it was Cubist; I liked that word.

I liked to draw, too. With my birthday money I bought books called *How to Draw Horses* and *How to Draw Cats,* and practiced following the numbered diagrams. But I couldn't seem to progress from making circles and ovals and triangles to making pictures that looked anything like cats and horses; I could not close the gap between what I imagined and what I could actually produce. There must be a trick that I did not yet know, some secret magic that maybe Trini would teach me. I was very proud that she liked me so much. I couldn't imagine anything I wanted more than for her and Daddy to get married. Still, I was a little bit surprised, because I had always thought she belonged with someone else.

Gordon was another friend of my parents, an old friend they knew from college, from before they were married. He had a round face and not much hair. He played the guitar and sang, which was not such a common thing in the early fifties as it would become in another ten years. He had a nice tenor voice, and knew lots of songs: *Jimmie Crack Corn, and I Don't Care. The Foggy, Foggy*

Dew. He sang songs from the Spanish Civil War: *Ay, Manuela!* He brought his guitar and sang at all my parents' parties, when we all still lived together — and he always came with Trini. They were Gordon-and-Trini, a single word. And now, as the wind whipped my hair — but not hurting too much, because I was in the front seat beside him — my father was talking about marrying Trini.

I was too young to calculate. I smiled and nodded my head up and down and said, "I would like that." I don't think Annie understood enough to say anything. We had to stop at the big store where Daddy bought all the little metal things he used for his work. Annie and I were so bored we started making a fuss and he yelled at us. Later, he cooked dinner and read us a story from *Russian Fairy Tales* before we went to sleep on the couch-pillows on the floor in our room that was like a front porch.

In the morning Annie and I went in to Daddy's room to wake him up for breakfast. Trini was there, sleeping next to him in his bed. "Oh!" I said. "I didn't know you were spending the night with us." They smiled and got up and Daddy made pancakes for breakfast. We were all happy. Daddy read us the funnies in his funny voices, and Trini laughed too. Then we went for a ride in the hills. I was so happy I didn't even mind sitting in the back seat with Annie. Up on Skyline, Daddy stopped the car and we walked through a gate into a field and sat down under a live-oak tree. Trini had brought a sketch pad. When she was drawing, she didn't want me to watch over her shoulder. She said she was just doodling. I don't think she ever drew people, only things like trees and sky and furniture.

When we got back home, Daddy and Trini had drinks. He made the drinks. I wanted to make martinis so Trini could see I knew how, but they had whisky instead. I was probably being a pest, because Trini told Daddy to make us drinks, too. He poured tonic water in our glasses and put in a squeeze of lemon and some of the red, sugary juice from the jar of cherries, and then we each got one cherry even though I asked for two. Trini started reading us a Baba Yaga story from the *Russian Fairy Tales* book, all of us piled together on Daddy's bed.

It was late in the afternoon, about the time we would have been having dinner if we'd been at my mother's house, but Daddy hadn't even started cooking yet. He and Trini were sitting close together while Trini was reading. Suddenly there was a big noise at the door, loud knocking that kept pounding and pounding, and then Gordon came in. He burst into the room. He shouted at Trini. "Your mother's been worried half to death about you!" He grabbed her arm and pulled her up off the bed. I scrambled for the book so our place wouldn't get lost.

My father yelled "Hey!" There was more yelling, and before I knew it, Gordon and Daddy were in the middle of the room punching each other, and Trini was crying and screaming, "Stop it! Stop it!" and trying to get between them, and Annie and I squashed up together on the bed. Annie's eyes, blue as Daddy's, filled with big tears as she cried: "Daddy! Daddy!"

Gordon and Daddy punched and shoved and crashed around the room. Hanging from the light fixture in the middle of the ceiling was a cardboard bird I'd made at school. It was supposed to be a peacock but it really looked more like a turkey, except that I had colored the tail feathers the color called "peacock blue" and made a gold eye in the middle of each one. I had made it for Daddy's new house, and now Gordon and Daddy crashed into it and set it swinging wildly back and forth, flying like a real bird. One hard push from someone — I don't remember who — and it fell, knocked into the corner. It reminded me of the nightmare I'd had over and over before the divorce, the-house-is-falling-down, and then I started crying too, even though I knew I was too big.

Finally the fight stopped and Gordon and Trini left. We probably ate something for supper before Daddy took us home. When I told my mother what happened, she said that was the way men argued, by hitting each other. And a few months later I heard that Gordon and Trini got married and moved away, and I was mad, because she should have married my father. I had wished for something, I had relaxed into the sureness that it was bound to happen, yet it hadn't. Once again, the world of the grownups had proved incomprehensible and disappointing.

Daddy only lived in the Loma Verde house for a few more months before he moved again, to a cottage in a prettier place, on Alpine Road. One night he took Annie and me to an Alec Guiness movie at the drive-in. It was a long summer evening, and the movie couldn't start until dark, so on a stage under the screen in the twilight, a magician performed some tricks. Everyone was out of their cars, standing in front of the stage to watch. I knew the tricks were only tricks; Daddy told me there was no such thing as magic. But I was spellbound as the magician pulled first one, then three, then a long, tied-together chain of bright silk squares from the palm of his hand. He juggled balls that disappeared into thin air. He called a little boy to come up on stage and pulled another long chain of scarves from his ear. I was jealous of that boy.

The magician asked for another volunteer, and I waved my hand wildly, and magically he chose me to come up to help him, and I climbed up to the stage. The sun was beginning to sink, and behind where all the people were standing, the windshields of the cars sparkled in the falling light as if they were covered with gold. When the magician asked me if I knew how to make chicken soup, I was suddenly too shy to speak. I didn't know how to make chicken soup, even though Daddy was teaching me to make crepes Suzette and martinis. The magician asked me what was the first thing I would need. Still tongue-tied, feeling my face glowing red as the sun-ball on the horizon, I shook my head.

"A chicken, right?" He spoke more to the audience than to me, but I nodded. From under his table, he brought out a big cooking pot, took the lid off, and waved the pot around, turning it upside down and shaking it to show everyone it was empty. He showed me, too, making sure I looked deep inside before telling him no, there was nothing in there. Then he put the lid back on and shook the pot madly up and down and all around and gave it to me to shake too. He said some magic words, took off the lid again — and there was a live bird inside! It was a pigeon, not a chicken, but still, it was a wonderful trick.

It was the last trick before the movie. The top edge of the sun was just dipping below the horizon. The magician said I could keep the pigeon, for being such a good helper, and he gave me a cardboard box to keep it in until we got home. All through the movie, squeezed between Annie and Daddy on the front seat, I thought about my magic bird sleeping in the box in the back seat, its wings sparkling with tiny rainbows of iridescence. Even though he'd made a face about it, Daddy promised he'd build a cage so I could keep the bird at his house. The movie was funny, and Daddy laughed a lot, but I was too excited about my prize to pay much attention. Annie fell asleep, leaning heavily against me. I tried to shove her away without Daddy noticing.

I liked to ride in the car in the mysterious night. The lights of the other cars made swirling patterns on the ceiling inside, and outside was the night world, the world the grownups had to themselves when children were asleep.

"What kind of cage will you make?" I asked.

Daddy cleared his throat. "You know," he said. "That pigeon would be a lot happier if we just let it go."

I didn't say anything. Inside the box on the backseat was my souvenir of magic. I could still remember my surprise, on the stage as the sun's setting light made everything look red — surprise and delight at seeing the pigeon in the pot. And yet I, wasn't surprised, because I knew there must be some point to the magician's trick. I still wanted to keep the pigeon, but I knew it wouldn't make any difference if I said so.

Your Fortune: Love and Marriage

Louis Borosov had a print shop downtown on High Street, off Lytton, a block from the Palo Alto *Times* building. It was in a little yellow house that looked from the outside like a home where a family might live. But inside it was a noisy, inky-stinky place crammed with stuff. There was a tiny front office with a counter where the customers came to leave and pick up their orders, and behind that, the shop itself, crowded with machinery, wooden cases of lead slugs and shelves of different kinds of paper.

Louis was my mother's boyfriend. He was a large man who towered over my little mother, but not at all in a threatening way. He was more like a big, soft pillow. His voice was soft, too, drifting from the side of his thin-lipped mouth like cigarette smoke. A long fringe of thin gray hair surrounded the bald top of his head. "No grass grows on a busy street," he chuckled, rubbing his pate and muttering something to my mother that I couldn't quite hear, something that made her blush.

The first time I saw the shop was when my mother brought me and Annie by when we were downtown buying new school clothes, just before I started fourth grade. Louis looked up when we came in; he smiled, happy to see us. He wore a blue apron with big pockets. He kissed my mother and introduced us to Tamara and George, who worked for him. George didn't look up from his machine until Louis tapped him on the shoulder; that was because he was deaf.

Louis cleared a pile of papers from a chair for my mother to sit, with Annie on her lap. He found a high stool for me and placed it in front of the linotype. I climbed up, dangling my feet in my new brown shoes. My socks were slipping down. The linotype had big, flat, square keys like Louis's flat, square fingers: ETAOINSHRDLU. Louis stretched out my small hands over the keys, like a piano teacher, and I found the letters to spell out my name. Louis pushed another key and pulled a lever, and from the noise and smell of the machinery a shiny lead slug with my name on it — backwards! — popped out like a soda bottle from a vending machine. Annie's fingers were too small, so I made one for her with her name on it, too. I was thrilled, pressing my fingers on the big keys, making something real.

"You must have printers' ink in your veins," Louis teased, with a little close-lipped smile. He slurred his words together; my mother always complained that he mumbled. I had no more trouble understanding him than I did other grownups — they all teased me with mysterious new words and sly smiles. But I had an idea of what it meant to have printers' ink in my veins. I liked it, and I begged and wheedled my way back to the print shop as often as I could.

Louis had begun to visit us soon after we moved to Windermere Street, after my parents got divorced. I was still in agony and grief over the loss of my father and my mother's apparent loss of sanity. I liked Louis because he was calm and slow, and because he treated me almost like a grownup, and because he made my mother happy. Her eyes were soft whenever he was around and she didn't yell so much. He brought us all presents from the print shop: stationery and rubber stamps and cocktail napkins with our names printed in different colors and typefaces. He brought us two fluffy black kittens and showed us how they would lick ice cream from our fingers. Louis brought the ice cream, too. And sometimes he brought his son, Lance, who was ten. We might have lost my father, but we had gained a new way of looking at life, my mother and I. She had Louis, and I had Lance.

When Louis brought Lance to our house, it was even better than the print shop. Lance and I sat close together on the floor, listening to records. I had my own phonograph that my father had built for me, and a few albums of 78 rpm records with booklets to read along. My favorite was "Tubby the Tuba," a little babyish for Lance. He brought his own favorite — "One String Fiddle," about a boy who made a kind of banjo out of a cigar box. I was allowed to play some of my mother's records too — Burl Ives, Marais and Miranda, Spike Jones. Sometimes we played Chinese checkers. I knew Lance would not care about my dolls, so I showed him the city plans and street maps I had drawn on long rolls of butcher paper, and the little cars I made from rectangular pink erasers with thumb tacks stuck in their sides for wheels. I wanted Lance to love me.

Love was always on my mind. I did not like being a little girl; it seemed a condition of hopeless powerlessness, like what I had learned about slavery. I imagined that true love would be my emancipation. I would be tenderly held in strong, loving arms and dance in the moonlight to swelling strings, with the sound of pounding surf in the distance. I didn't yet know his name, but I knew I would know him when I saw him, and we would fall in love. We would get married; I would have a new name, and become someone else. We would have four children, two boys and two girls. I was always trying to think of matching names for them, like Jamie, Joanna, Judy and Joe.

Where were my mother and Louis when Lance and I were playing together, all those afternoon hours? They were in my mother's room with the door closed. Lance said we'd better not bother them. He turned over the record for the next chapter of "One String Fiddle," and I drew trees along the streets of my butcher-paper city. When Annie woke up from her nap I was supposed to let her play with us. I hoped she would sleep until my mother and Louis came out. I wanted to keep Lance for myself. Annie was too little to appreciate him.

Louis and I had our bonds — we both loved cats, and the smell of printers' ink — but they were nothing to the bond I could sense between him and my mother, the aura that glowed around them as they sat close on the couch, drinking martinis, murmuring together while I played with the kittens or squabbled with Annie. Their connection absorbed and fascinated me. I could not wait to grow up so that a man would look at me like that.

I dreamed that Lance was my true love. When we were grown up, we'd dance together in the light of a full moon. He would kiss me, hold me close, whisper: "Darling, I love you." For our wedding I would wear a beautiful long white dress with a veil, and a train held up by two adorable little children, and after the ceremony we would walk out of the church under the crossed swords of his comrades. Lance was a day student at Palo Alto Military Academy; he wanted to go to West Point someday. I was only a little troubled by his militarism, even though I was for peace, not war. My parents were for peace. Yet I knew from the example of my mother and Louis, that true love could overcome political differences. "Louis is a Republican!" my mother told her friends in a shocked tone — but she laughed about it, too.

One New Year's Eve, Louis came over with a bottle of Mumm's champagne, and Annie and I got to have sips. We were going to stay up until midnight to see in the new year. Louis had brought another surprise, something even my mother had never heard of. He had brought a box of lead slugs from the print shop, and after an argument with my mother about which pot he could use, he melted the lead on our stove while my mother filled a bucket with cold water and emptied both trays of ice cubes into it and brought it to the living room, where Annie and I had spread newspapers on the floor.

"Watch out! Stand back!" Louis carefully carried the pan of molten lead in from the kitchen. Annie and I stood back. It was a little scary and hard to understand, but fun, too. Like our mother and Louis.

Louis held his hands over mine on the pot handle, and guided me to pour out a bit of melted lead into the bucket. *Hissss!* A cloud of steam rose as the molten metal hit the ice water and quickly hardened into a strange, jagged lump. Then it was Annie's turn, and then my mother and Louis each poured. One, two, three, four — one lead chunk for each of us.

"What is it?" Annie and I both cried. The process had been dramatic, but the results were only dull pieces of metal junk.

Louis laughed his soft, slightly mocking laugh. "It's your fortune," he said, as if we should have known. "You tell me what it is. It's like a Rorschach test." He winked at my mother.

"Yes, a Rorschach," she laughed.

I knew what that was — it was a test my mother gave to her patients, and I had tried it myself. There were cards with inkblots on them and you said what they made you think of. My blob of lead didn't make me think of anything. I was disappointed. I needed to know my fortune! Would Lance and I get married? Maybe before I got married, I would be a movie actress, like Natalie Wood. Or a writer. I couldn't see any of that in this misshapen gray clod.

"Mine is some kind of animal!" Mother's voice held more

excitement than I thought was deserved. Louis growled playfully at her.

But we had fun even if I didn't understand my fortune. It was still a happy evening, with the thrill of the champagne, and staying up until midnight. My mother was happy. Louis sang "Auld Lang Syne" and we joined in. The words reminded me of the "Ollie Ollie Oxen Free" that signaled the end of hide-and-seek, when I never quite ran fast enough to get back to the base without being tagged.

What did those lead shapes mean? We might not have been able to read them, but in the beginning of summer, as soon as the school year was over, we moved from Windermere Street to a tract house at the other end of town, in South Palo Alto. The development was named "Fairmeadow," a hopeful promise. My mother's friends helped us move, and I carried Goldie the Goldfish in her bowl on my lap in the car. On the next trip we brought Cindy and Gatita, the kittens Louis had given us, now grown into fluffy black cats. But Louis was nowhere to be found.

I asked my mother what happened to him. "He wanted to get married!" She said it as if it were an impossible demand, something unforgivably wrong. I asked her why that meant they had to break up — why things couldn't just go on as they were? She sighed and said I was too young to understand. She told me not to cry about it, but I was thinking that I would never see Lance again.

2.

One late summer afternoon, just before I started the eighth grade, Louis Borosov brought my mother home and re-entered our lives. Mother looked smaller than usual; she was pale and tense. She had been in a car accident on the four-lane highway she drove back and forth to work every day, the road everyone called Bloody Bayshore.

We hadn't seen Louis in a few years, but he was the person she had called when she needed someone. She looked helpless, but somehow happy, leaning against his shoulder. He would take care of everything. He would have spoken with the police and had the wreck towed away, he would call the insurance company and go with her to buy a new car. My mother always said it was better to have a man along for those kinds of things.

My mother worked in a mental health clinic in San Mateo, about twenty miles away. She complained a lot about having to work so hard, but she was proud of it, too. When I talked about being an actress or a writer, she shook her head and told me to find a good man to take care of me and make me happy.

Louis had the appearance of being that kind of good man, substantial and steady. He took us out to dinner at fancy restaurants where he liked to hear my mother talk to the waiters in French. I didn't realize that we ate for free because Louis printed the menus and matchbooks and business cards for the restaurants. I was certainly too young to know that a man who owned his own print shop wasn't necessarily rich.

I was happy to see Louis again. I hoped my mother had changed her mind about marrying him. I looked forward to a wedding at which I could secretly rehearse for my own. Annie could be the flower girl and I could be a junior bridesmaid. I wouldn't even mind wearing matching dresses, for once. My father had remarried the previous year, but only in the county courthouse, and we children had not been invited. I felt cheated by his plain announcement, the lack of romance or drama. That was his style. But my mother loved big parties and fancy dresses; she and Louis would certainly have a real wedding. And Lance, who was away at boarding school, would surely be there.

Many of the familiar signs of Louis' presence began to reappear in our house: the personalized napkins and matchbooks, the beautiful cut-glassware that had been his mother's; the restaurant-quality kitchen gadgets, like a meat-slicer and an ice-crushing blender. And Louis himself, his soft bulk and his low, mumbling voice, his bad French that made my mother roll her eyes. He liked to pretend to talk French with my mother, just like he'd always put the French accents on her name when he printed it on napkins or matchbooks. She didn't really like the things with her name printed on them — she was always complaining about his presents. But he took us all to the movies and bought popcorn. Best of all, he held my mother's interest and drew it away from me. I had already reached the age when I found her attention oppressive.

I had decided I wanted to change myself before the next year of school started. I did not want to be the girl I had been in seventh grade: a watcher of happy, going-steady couples pressing each other close during slow dances, holding hands with fingers interlaced as they walked through the halls between classes. I wanted the feelings the songs on the radio were about: *you're mine, never let me go, I will love you forever.* I wanted to wear a boy's St. Christopher medal around my neck so everyone would know we were going steady. And I knew I looked all wrong — I still looked like a little girl. I studied teen magazines and eavesdropped on the popular girls in the bathroom. I noticed what they were wearing. I bought white lipstick and brushed and dressed my short hair into a perky duck-tail in the back. I dropped my bike riding, badminton-playing playmates. They were childish; I was embarrassed to be seen with them now.

I liked a boy in my art class. His name was Dean Gamble; his dark hair was gently Brylcreemed and his skin almost perfectly clear. I liked his clothes: neat chinos and pale blue or yellow oxford shirts, open at the collar. I always liked the tall boys. He had a slow, lazy way about him, and I imagined his voice would be slow and lazy too. I had to imagine it; I had never heard him speak.

In art class we sat on tall stools at long tables. While we drew and painted, Mr. Larsen played records, soft jazz or semi-classical pieces. Our first assignment was to make a one-word sign, choosing an appropriate lettering style. I wrote the word CATS giving the C little ears and whiskers, and turning the S into a sinuous tail, with a cat's body perched on top. Dean wrote CARS in low, wide, feathered letters that seemed to speed across the paper on their wheels. Because our words were similar, Mr. Larsen posted our signs next to each other on the bulletin board. I thought Dean smiled at me. I thought I might see him at the dance.

We had school dances on the first Friday evening of every month. I planned what I was going to wear two weeks in advance, down to every piece of underwear. As I soaked in a tub of scented bubbles, I listened to the radio. Pat Boone, The Four Aces, Dorothy McGuire translated the raw rhythm and blues I heard late at night on the Negro station from Oakland. There was a whiny country thread, too, in some of the music I liked: Faron Young, Patsy Cline, Ferlin Husky. All of it was the music of love, the songs of kisses and promises and heartbreak: the grownup world.

Over layers of petticoats that I'd spent days washing and starching, I set my circle skirt, pale pink with a cheery embroidered poodle. I had a matching pink short-sleeved angora sweater. I carefully straightened the dark seams of my new nylons and clipped the tops to the garters at the bottom of my panty- girdle. I had flat pink shoes to match the skirt. I sprayed myself with "Chantilly," the same sweet, flowery fragrance as the bubble bath and dusting powder I'd used. I hoped Dean would like it.

When I was finally ready, I came into the kitchen. Over the sound of my radio I'd heard my mother come home, and then, about a half hour later, I heard Louis. When I came out, they were having drinks in the kitchen while the dinner finished cooking. Louis looked me up and down, and made me turn around to make sure my stocking seams were straight. He examined my nails; he had shown me just a few weeks before how to use the mother-of-pearl handled manicure set my grandmother had given me.

I had to eat carefully so I wouldn't spill anything on my sweater, but my emotions were in too much turmoil for me to eat very much anyway. I began to worry about whether Dean would come to the dance at all — some boys didn't go to dances. I was trying to remember the things I'd read in magazines about how to be popular with boys. Ask him what kind of car he likes best, I thought. I kept looking at the clock on the stove. The dance started at seven.

"Why don't you drive her, Louis," my mother asked, sipping her drink.

Louis had a silly way of bowing. *"Mais oui,"* he said.

I didn't want Louis to tease me, so I struggled to suppress my high state of excitement. My blood was racing. Tonight, tonight, would be the night for me. Dean would see me from across the room and stride purposefully forward, extending his hand to me, looking into my eyes. "May I have this dance?" he would ask. He wouldn't let me go for the rest of the evening. Our admiring and envious classmates would part to make a circle around us as we bopped to The Big Bopper and The Coasters. Then we'd slowly glide around the floor to "Earth Angel," pressing our cheeks close together when the chaperones weren't watching. "Darling, I love you," he would whisper in my ear — the magic words that would fly me to womanhood, and happiness.

The cafetorium — our school's multi-purpose room — was decorated with crepe paper and balloons in fall colors, and the tables and chairs had been removed except for a few chairs left at the edges of the room. I noticed that the only girls sitting down were the ones considered hopelessly outcaste. I stood gingerly at the edge of the floor. The first couples to dance were the ones who were already going steady. The rest of us hovered at the edges.

Across the room I spied Dean. He was talking with another boy as his eyes scanned the room. I smiled bravely. He would come to me; I was sure. I was thinking about the ball in *War and Peace*, and I felt just like Natasha, wondering if I had made a huge mistake to come at all. And then, just when she's about to give up, Prince Andrey walks towards her, smiling, telling her he's so happy to see her: "May I have the honor?" My grandmother thought I looked like Audrey Hepburn.

A few feet away from me, Patty Purcell and Abby Tomasini giggled together in their full, gingham skirts, Patty in green, Abby in blue. Their hair was styled in identical perfect page-boys, the ends rolled stylishly up — Patty's blonde, Abby's dark. I turned away quickly, not to be caught looking at them, but as I turned, I saw Dean walking across the room to take Patty's hand and lead her to the center of the floor.

A boy did ask me to dance, finally, but it was just Norman Wirtz, short and plain, from my AP English class. We danced slowly to the Platters' "The Great Pretender," while I struggled not to take the lead. He moved stiffly, in dancing-school steps, holding me at a respectable distance. I caught a glimpse of Dean, holding little blonde Patty Purcell close to his chest, his eyes squeezed shut in ecstasy as they shuffled together in slow circles. Norman and I did not talk; he seemed as relieved as I was when our dance was over.

I could not leave. Louis would come to pick me up at exactly 9:30. I would be expected to tell him what a good time I'd had. I was too proud to run to the girls' bathroom and cry; it would be filled with gossiping girls sneaking cigarettes, girls who would ask me what was wrong, who I liked, proffering advice or veiled taunts.

The evening wore on. I danced twice more, with different boys, both short, both dull. When they played "Goodnight, Irene," the dance was over. I tried not to look at the kids who left in couples, especially Dean and Patty.

I found Louis' Plymouth outside and got into the seat beside him. The cigarette smell was strong, and the other funny smell he and my mother often had on their breath. He gave me a wry, appraising look: "So, how was it?"

"OK," I said. It was starting to drizzle, and Louis had the windshield wipers on. He looked tired, and that was fine with me. I didn't feel like talking. He looked sideways at me.

"Well, m'dear, things are tough all over," he said. It was what he always said to me and Annie when we complained about anything. It wasn't fair, I hadn't even complained. I hated the expression, and it was worse in front of my mother, because she always laughed in a mean way. I didn't answer him. I was afraid if I opened my mouth I'd start to cry.

A couple of weeks later, Louis took me with him on an errand. He had some menus to deliver at a French restaurant just outside of town, on El Camino. Louis drove in the fast lane with only his right hand on the wheel, his left arm resting on the open window. Outside the city limits, El Camino was lined with shabby businesses — a used car lot, a motel, a couple of gas stations, an antique store in a building that looked like an old barn.

There was a small, square building, painted dark pink that

I noticed whenever I passed it. Outside was a blue wooden sign on a sandwich board, showing the outline of a hand. Over the hand in big white letters was the word: PALMIST. At the bottom of the sign, the same white letters, slightly smaller, read: LOVE MONEY PAST PRESENT FUTURE. Once I had asked my mother to stop so that I could have my palm read, but she made a face and didn't even slow down.

Chez Pierre was a low, white building with blue shutters and a red door, and a French flag flying from a flagpole. Louis pulled into the parking lot. He liked to have a drink or two with the owner; he didn't mind if I wandered off to have my fortune told. The gypsy house was only a few hundred yards down the road. Louis gave me an ironic smile and waved me off.

It was warm and windy, early afternoon. I walked on the side of the highway, kicking up dust, my sockless feet sliding in soft black flats. I had about seven dollars with me, my allowance and some baby-sitting money, in my black plastic purse. My heart was thumping, and I could feel my underarms wet under my blue tunic top as I got closer to the gypsy house. It was exotic and scary, but there were things I needed to know. What was in my future? Was anyone ever going to fall in love with me? Would there be tender kisses and slow dances, a beautiful bridal gown and veil, sunny children gathered around me? Would my face ever be on the big screen, my name on the marquee, my books in the bookstore? The gypsy's door was ajar, with a cowbell hung to ring if it was moved the slightest bit. I stood outside and wiped my hands on my black capri pants. I looked at my palms: the lines and pads that told me no more than that I was a human being.

The cowbell jangled when I touched the door. I pushed it open and entered a dark, airless room. My eyes made out a round table and two kitchen chairs. I swallowed hard, quiet, waiting. A fat woman, swaddled in layers of shawls and scarves, came out of a room behind.

"What you want?" Her voice was harsh.

I spoke up, shaky, but brave. "How much is it to have my palm read?"

She turned away.

"You too young!"

Too young? How could someone be too young to have a future? To want to know her fortune? I was still with disbelief.

She turned back toward me, and for a moment I thought she was changing her mind.

"Go! You go now!"

Now I was scared. I turned, stumbling a little, and ran back to Chez Pierre.

Louis was standing in front of his car, smoking.

"Well, m'dear? Did you find out what you wanted to know?"

I shook my head and got into the car. "How old do you have to be to have your palm read?" I demanded.

He laughed. "Old enough to know better," he said. It was a typical Louis answer.

Before the next dance, I had decided to change myself again. I had a new perfume, "Jungle Gardenia," which I had read in a movie magazine was Natalie Wood's favorite. I had new clothes: a straight black skirt and a green sweater with a deep V-neck. I had a new padded bra that my mother had snickered at, but paid for. I'd demanded it after one of the popular girls had called me a "carpenter's dream" — flat as a board.

Louis sniffed the air when I entered the kitchen in my cloud of sensual, tropical nights. He looked at me, nodding his approval. Did he joke that I looked "sexy" in my sweater and tight skirt?

Whatever he said or did — perhaps nothing, perhaps something completely unrelated to me — sent my mother into a rage. She yelled at him until he left, and then she drove me to the dance herself, silently.

I wasn't mooning over Dean Gamble any more. I was more relaxed, and maybe that was why more boys asked me to dance. Maybe it was my new look, or the "Jungle Gardenia." And then Ronnie Bowling, who wasn't in any of my classes, but who I'd admired in the halls, sauntered over. He flicked his eyes over me and extended his hand.

He had long, dark blond hair, elaborately combed and dressed with Vaseline so it cascaded in a long, twisty curl down the middle of his wide forehead. The back was formed into an ornate duck-tail, barely clearing his collar — the maximum length allowed by our school's dress code. Instead of chinos or corduroys, he wore jeans, low on his hips. He had long eyelashes and sleepy lids, and full, heavy lips. He didn't take art, he took auto shop. I thought he was adorable.

Ronnie didn't steer me around in a box-step like the other boys. He pulled me close, his right palm spread across the middle of my back, just over my bra hook. His left hand clasped my right tightly under his chin, which was so close to my temple that I could smell the spearmint-over-cigarette scent of his breath.

Slow, fast, slow. After "In the Still of the Night," came "Charlie Brown." We bopped in the twisty, toe-in way everyone did. But Ronnie's knees were bent deeper, his hips swung wide, back and forth, dangerously close to the forbidden "dirty bop." Gamely, I followed.

In the last slow dance, he held me even closer. His mouth moved towards my ear. I held my breath. "I think you're cute," he whispered.

It was not quite Prince Andrey, but I trembled.

Later that night, after she'd picked me up and we'd gone home, my mother told me she had broken up with Louis for good. She was having a drink when she told me this, and she was in a talky mood. She told me that after she'd broken up with Louis the first time, he'd married someone else, and then been divorced again.

And then it all came out: When Louis had first started seeing my mother, he'd still been married to Lance's mother, Artemis. And Artemis hadn't been Louis' first wife, but his third. And so Louis attained the dimensions of another of my heroines, Elizabeth Taylor, whose husbands' names I could easily recite: Nicky Hilton, Michael Wilding, Mike Todd, Eddie Fisher... I didn't know why this idea appealed to me so much, that marriage might be something to be done, and done, and done again. It was more mysterious than ever that my mother didn't want to get married at all. That once, to my father, had been enough.

3.

In the early nineteen-seventies, my mother married a man named Jim and moved to a beautiful modern house in Menlo Park, with a pool. All of us — Annie and I and our husbands and babies, Jim's kids and their wives and girlfriends, and all of our friends, spent a lot of time there during the warmer months. None of us, not even Jim and my mother, ever wore bathing suits. We lay in the sun and on floats in the pool, drinking cold drinks from plastic glasses and smoking pot. Toward evening, Jim would light some charcoal in the barbecue, and, warm and brown, we'd eat at the picnic table on the patio. In the seventies, we thought the world would be like this forever: paradise.

Then, a month or so after Peter left me, during a week when he had taken the kids to visit his parents, my mother called and asked if I wanted to come down for the weekend.

"Louis Borosov is coming to visit," she said. "I thought you might like to see him."

Louis Borosov! That was a name from the past.

"Where has he been?" I asked.

He had been living in Yucatan, and was back in the US to work for a couple of years to build up his Social Security account before he retired. He was bringing his Mexican wife.

"So, how many wives is this?" I asked.

My mother laughed. "Who knows?"

Louis was sitting at the picnic table next to the pool, wearing a short-sleeved shirt woven with a subtle Mexican pattern, drinking a tall scotch highball. His wife, Enriqueta, wore a black dress. They sat in the shade, and I was reminded of Louis' fair, thin, skin; how he had complained after taking us to the beach, years ago, that even the soles of his feet were sunburned.

Louis stood up when he saw me. He hugged me gently and mumbled something before he introduced me to Enriqueta. My mother had whispered hurriedly to me that she spoke no English; I realized that was partly why I had been invited, though my high-school Spanish was rough and poor.

I had rolled a joint and offered it around, but my mother was the only one who shared it. Louis laughed: "No thanks, m'dear," and Enriqueta waved it away, saying something I couldn't catch. Louis translated, "She says it's for arthritis," he said. "She knows all about that. She's a *bruja*." I gave her another look. I had read Carlos Casteneda.

"*Usted sabe de las yerbas?*" I asked, crudely. She answered with a string of fast Spanish, of which I could only understand the first word: *Si.* I shrugged, pathetically.

She looked intently at me. She and Louis conversed briefly in Spanish. Louis smiled softly and looked at me.

"She wants to know your astrological sign," he said.

"Pisces," I told her.

She took one of my hands from across the table. I hoped she was going to read my palm. I needed to know whether I would ever be happy again.

"*Pisces,*" she said, giving it the Spanish long "ee" sound. "*Tu poder es en tus manos.*"

Your power is in your hands.

I could translate the words, but I didn't know what they meant. I asked Louis to ask her if she would read my palm.

"My husband just left me," I said, offering my need.

She smiled. No, she did not read palms.

"*Cartas,*" she said. "*Solamente en las cartas.*"

"I have Tarot cards," I said, jumping up. I had brought them with me.

But when I handed her the cards she didn't read them for me. Instead she told me, partly herself and partly through Louis, how the cards she used were different: "*Cartas Españolas,*" older than my Waite-Rider designs. She explained how she prepared her cards specially, burning certain herbs whose names Louis could not translate, spreading the cards out under the light of the old moon.

"He wants to come back to you," she said suddenly, in heavily accented English. "But you don't want him."

I shrugged. I didn't think that was true, but I didn't know.

My mother had gone inside to start preparing things for dinner, and Enriqueta went in, too, to take a nap. Louis looked like he was napping over his drink. It was not as warm a day as

I'd thought it would be, but the pool was still inviting. I smoked a little more pot and walked to the edge, stripped, and slipped into the water. It was slightly heated and very comfortable. I swam a few gentle laps and then floated on my back, looking up at the pattern the limbs of the live-oak made against the sky. It was strange; I was usually here with the children; I missed their noise and splash.

Jim came home with groceries and charcoal briquets and began to start the barbecue. My mother was making shish kebab, a specialty. I was looking forward to dinner.

The year before, my mother and Jim had gone to Europe, and my mother brought me a length of silk from Italy. It was beautiful fabric, a pale blue with a pattern of soft rose and gold flowers. There wasn't quite enough of it to make a real dress, but I'd made it into a short sarong, and when I had dried off from my swim, that's what I put on.

I was on my way back into the house to see if my mother needed any help. Louis still looked like he was napping, but as I passed him, he reached out toward me. His hand grazed over my behind and down the outside of my thigh. "A man would have to be crazy to leave you," he murmured.

I blushed and hoped that no one else had heard him. I was ashamed of the way my heart jumped to hear it. I knew I should be angry and offended. I was a feminist, not a sex-object. He was more than twice my age! He was married! *He had been my mother's boyfriend!* He was a dirty old man, but he was also Louis, who had held my small fingers over the linotype keys. And I knew he — like his new wife — was trying to save me, to give me hope that all love was not dead and gone. When I smiled at him, it was a reflection of his own wry, bemused smile.

The Sea Is Awash With Roses

It was a little after nine in the morning when I heard that Jerry Garcia was dead. It was a news bulletin that broke into the show I was watching. I yelled "Shut up!" at the TV and then I called Willy. He was asleep and he didn't know yet. I had to tell him, but I didn't have to say more than "It's Jerry, I just heard on TV" and he said, "Oh, no," in a soft, sleepy voice. We were both quiet for a minute. Then he said, "Well, dad-rat it," and we both kind of laughed.

More than thirty years earlier, Willy had come to my high school at the morning break. He'd waited for me by the donut counter in front of the cafetorium to tell me that our friend Paul Speegle was dead. Paul was another weird high school kid, like me — only he wasn't just weird, he was a real artist, a painter. He'd even had a show in a gallery in North Beach. He was supposed to be somebody, but he and a bunch of other people — Jerry had been one of them — were speeding through the hills out by the new VA hospital and spun out, off the road.

Now I told Willy I'd come over to his place later. I had errands, or at least I thought I did. I went to the farmers' market but I couldn't remember what I'd gone for, so I drove over the bridge to San Rafael. Willy wasn't home. His truck was gone, and I could hear the phone ringing inside and nobody answering, so I left a note in his mailbox and drove back home.

The summer before my last year in high school I volunteered to work at the Peace Center. It was an old house near the Stanford campus, with a meeting room downstairs and rooms upstairs that were rented out. I parked my bike and went in, and there was this guy sitting on the floor cross-legged. That was Willy: reading a newspaper and smoking a Lucky Strike. His bright red beard shone like a firebrand and lit my teenage heart. He had a beautiful smile. I was sixteen and he was twenty-one.

That summer we painted the Peace Center and marched to San Quentin to protest capital punishment. This was before Vietnam; Kennedy and Nixon were running for president. The Peace Center was for disarmament and stopping nuclear tests. Some people there were working for a federated world government. Willy wrote a newsletter that he sent to all kinds of important people, whether they asked for it or not.

The fall came wet and rainy, and the winter was wetter, and we spent most of our time in Willy's room upstairs at the Peace Center, listening to the rain and Brahm's First Symphony. Willy had painted his walls purple and found a straw-seated wooden chair like the one Van Gogh painted in his room in Arles. A door laid flat across a pair of sawhorses was his desk, covered in piles of books and papers, and more paper always spilling out of his typewriter. Books filled the brick-and-board shelves against the walls and teetered in stacks on the floor. There was a narrow bed with a scratchy woolen blanket, where we spent the most time of all.

We read Kenneth Patchen to each other: *The sea is awash with roses, O they blow upon the land ...* and *O my darling troubles heaven with her loveliness ...* One day Willy surprised me, picking me up after school in a 1938 Dodge sedan: he had a car! We named it Karma and I picked weedy wildflowers from the Peace Center yard and put them in the car's little vases. We started going out more; we went to see *Black Orpheus* and *The Umbrellas of Cherbourg*.

A few days after the car crash that killed Paul, Willy brought me to a shabby apartment building in East Palo Alto to meet some new people he'd met. Jerry was sitting on the floor noodling on a guitar. His arm was still in a cast; he'd broken it in the crash. There were two or three other guys there, smoking and making dry jokes.

These were Willy's new friends, and we started hanging out with them. We sat in Kepler's bookstore, where they had an espresso bar and Turkish pastries. Ken Kesey held court at a table there, wearing a captain's hat, leaning back in his chair. We had our own table. Jerry and Bob Hunter — who I knew from junior high — and some other guys played guitars and sang folk songs and blues. If we weren't at Kepler's, we hung out at St. Michael's Alley, a new coffee house in downtown Palo Alto, until the owner kicked us out.

I turned seventeen in March, with a big, wild party at the Peace Center that would have gotten Willy evicted if the people who ran it hadn't been Quakers and willing to talk about it. I was bursting with juicy life, and there were plenty of other places to have parties. We rode in caravans, back and forth from the Negro neighborhood in East Palo Alto we called The Ghetto to an old mansion in the hills at the end of a long driveway lined with live-oaks and oleanders. Hunter and another guy we knew rented rooms there, and Jerry and some other people lived in cars parked in the driveway. We called it the Chateau. In the late afternoon, the sun gleamed on the dried out lawn and the carpet of fallen leaves, and Frank, who might have owned the place, would throw darts at a board hung on a tree and drink beer from a six pack at his feet. He had an old body-builder's body gone to fat, his belly drooping over his leopard-skin bikini trunks.

I was off with the wraggle-taggle gypsies-O. Besides the musicians and the crazy chicks who liked to hang out with them, there were misfit high school kids and drop outs, and a few rare birds, like Alan, with his classy English accent, who'd come to Palo Alto with his father, a scholar at the Ford Foundation. The wine flowed from big Red Mountain jugs; blue smoke hung in the air. Around eleven, the jazz people would come and set up. Ronnie Mann, ivory pale and skinny as a stick, hunched over his sax in a corner. Jackson, porkpie-hatted trumpet player, theatrical in the best fifties jazz style: "Mayhaps one of you might convey me to Berrone's, where I might procure some peppermint schnapps ..." Berrone's was a big liquor store at the end of University Avenue, just past the two-mile dry zone around the Stanford campus. A high school kid named Danny played drums, and there was another kid, even younger — a spade, as we said then — who blew such a great sax they took him up to the City with them to jam in after-hours clubs.

Hippie was still a bad word then, a word we used to put people down — people who weren't cool; people who snapped their fingers too much and read bad poetry. Sometime that spring we started calling ourselves the Love Scene. It might have been David X who first named it that, or maybe it was someone else. Many of us had monikers by then: Party John, Pogo, Two-Buttons, John the Poet, David X. I named David X, and in return he named me, Saeda Dawoud, but nobody except him ever called me that. We were renaming everything but we hardly paid attention to what we were doing. We were not very self-conscious; we were just having a good time, doing what we liked. I liked to get drunk at parties and go around and kiss everyone. "I love you," I'd say, as I kissed each one. It drove Willy crazy, and after a while, things like that broke us up.

I thought about all that as I drove back home from Willy's empty house the day Jerry died. There were messages on my phone machine. One from my best girl friend in high school, who'd lived with Jerry for awhile, after I went to New York. One from my son, who'd caught the news on the Internet. One from Willy, saying he was home. He'd just been out to take his daughter to the bus stop.

I talked to Willy on the phone two or three times that afternoon. Talking to him made me lonely, though, so about six in the evening I drove back to his place in San Rafael. It had been a hot day, and it was still hot. On the way out of the house I grabbed two bottles of Guinness out of the refrigerator.

Willy was sitting in a plastic chair on the concrete porch in front of his house, smoking a cigarette. I bent down to hug him and we both cried a little. He's a big man now, with a belly that looks like a seven-month pregnancy. He has a big square head and short gray hair. I handed him a beer. "It's cooler out back," he said, getting up.

The back yard was neat, grass mowed and trees trimmed, but everything looked a little dead. There was a small shed there, half-attached to the garage, padlocked. Willy moved a red plastic mat and lay down on it. I sat on the edge of a step.

"This reminds me of Paul Speegle," I said. "We always seem to be telling each other somebody's dead. It's, like, our whole relationship."

I wasn't just talking about the day Willy had come to my high school to tell me about Paul. Over the years, a lot of the folks we knew were gone, and Willy had called to tell me about most of them: Pigpen McKernan, whose mother used to come to shows at Frost. Phil and Party John's friend Bobby Petersen, who'd visited me once in New York and brought me a huge box of peyote buttons. Ronnie Mann, who called me from prison so often I finally went to visit him there. Lester Hellums, who sold me a terrible tape of his jazz group for ten dollars, just a few months before he died.

Willy laughed. There was a gang tag painted on one of the posts in back of the house and Willy told me his daughter's friends came over, and a bunch of boys came over; all the kids were smoking pot and drinking and making out, and Willy finally got mad because they were trying to get him to unlock the shed. "I let her see some of my rage," he said.

Ronnie Mann had a shed like that in the back yard of the house where he lived with his wife Genie and their three little children, just on the edge of the ghetto, in Menlo Park. After I broke up with Willy, I used to meet Party John there and drink sloe gin fizzes and smoke joints Ronnie sold us for fifty cents. John and I would go in the shed and make love. I didn't say anything to Willy about that now, though, because even after all those years I didn't know how he'd react. He probably knew all about it anyway.

"Would you like to go to the Mayflower?" He asked. "Greasy food?"

"Sure," I said. "Do you want to wait for Margarite?" I wasn't very hungry.

"Oh, she'll probably call in sometime soon."

Margarite wasn't Willy's biological daughter, but he'd taken care of her since she was a toddler. Her parents had some connection with the band. They'd abandoned their kids for dope, and Margarite and her sister had been bounced around a bit. She was thirteen now and she'd been living with Willy full time for about four years. He'd jumped through all the county social services hoops and legally adopted her.

We went inside and I watched him feed Margarite's cat and then we got into his truck. When we were a couple of blocks away, he slowed down. Margarite was standing on the corner. I got out so she could climb in between us. She was wearing black lipstick and a lot of eyeliner. I wasn't sure if she'd bleached her hair or if it had always been that light.

The Mayflower is an English pub in downtown San Rafael. It has darts and a lot of different beers on tap and English pub food. Willy and I sat on one side of the table and Margarite sat across. When she picked up the menu I saw her long red and gold fingernails. I ordered a half order of fish and chips and a bottle of Red Tail. She ordered chicken wings and fries. Willy had a pasty and a Guinness. I got up to go to the ladies' room.

When I got back, they were both smoking. Margarite was looking funny at me, but I didn't know what I was supposed to do. Willy explained. "She wanted to know if it was all right to smoke in front of you," he said.

"What am I going to do?" I said to her. "Yell at you? I hate it, but it's not an age thing. I hate it when he does it, too."

"I was the last person she let smoke in her house," Willy said proudly.

"Did you know that Willy was my boyfriend when I was sixteen?" I asked Margarite.

That got the biggest reaction I'd seen from her all evening. Her eyes popped and her jaw went slack. Then she gave me a beautiful smile. *"Really?"*

We were all quiet. I knew she wanted to know why we weren't still together. I could have been her new mother. I didn't tell her I used to wear white lipstick back then, either. I didn't want her to lose respect for me.

"I wasn't ready for a serious relationship," I said.

I'd told Willy I'd love him forever, that I'd marry him as soon as I turned eighteen. We picked out names for our children. And then, abruptly, I'd fallen out of love. Suddenly, he wasn't as cool as I'd thought he was. I thought our new friends were cooler, with their wine and pills and jive talk. One night, like a lot of other nights, drunk on white port and lemon juice, I was going around the party kissing everybody.

Willy caught up with me and put his hand on my shoulder, gently. "I wish you wouldn't do that," he said.

"But I love everybody!" I was defiant. "This is the Love Scene, and I love everybody! I want to kiss everybody in the world!"

He stared, exasperated.

I turned my back on him and found someone else to kiss.

I felt Willy grab my arm and pull me away. And then he slapped me.

I was shocked, but that wasn't why I broke up with him. I broke up with him because I was seventeen and I wanted to have a good time. Because with all that noise about love, I really had no idea about love at all.

When I pulled the plug on us, Willy fell apart. It was a bad scene. He shaved off his beard, and people said he had flipped out. He wrote me letters, but I felt so guilty I couldn't even speak to him. When he was around I looked away from him. I ran around with the Love Scene on my own for a couple of weeks, and then I hooked up with Party John, and then the summer was over, and I left for New York to go to college.

Later, when I'd been away for a couple of year, Willy and I wrote a few letters back and forth. We never mentioned what had happened. He sent me a copy of the *I Ching*. Then we lost touch and I didn't see him again for almost twenty years. Jerry and the Grateful Dead were very famous by then, and Willy was working for them. One day I saw his name in the liner notes of a record album, and tracked him down through my friend Susan, who'd helped start *Rolling Stone* and knew famous rock and roll people. I sent a letter to an address Susan gave me, and a month later I came home to find Willy sitting in my living room.

He was wearing a suit and his big smile. He pointed at my daughter. "Why, she looks more like you than you do." He could still make me laugh. Even my husband was impressed. "His shoes were shined," he said later. "You can't fake that." There was never anything fake about Willy, not the least little thing, but I could never explain that.

He took us to shows and gave us backstage passes. At Frost Amphitheater, at Stanford, the old times and the new times came together in a blur for me. *It all rolls into one,* as they sang in "Stella Blue." When I was a little girl, I'd played on those terraced steps and rolled down the aisles to the bottom of the hill. I saw a flasher there once, when I was ten. And Jerry and the others in the band didn't forget their old friends, lots of people I knew from the old days were backstage, drinking beer and smoking. It was like a Love Scene party in a slightly different language, because of the things that hadn't changed, and the things that had. We were all older, for one thing. Pogo was in a wheelchair now. Laird showed up, wearing too many gold chains to be in any honest business.

Sometimes at shows when I walked through the crowd of tie-dyed, long-haired freaks I'd think a face was familiar, until I realized the friend I was remembering wasn't eighteen any more. And it was strange to hear Jerry's voice over the greatest sound system in the world, the same voice I'd listened to over a table of dirty coffee cups in Kepler's, on the lawn in front of the Chateau on a May afternoon, passing around a jug of Red Mountain, or in the City, sitting on the floor in an apartment on Noriega Street in the middle of a pile of empty Chinese food cartons. Backstage at those shows, I felt like I'd come home.

In the Mayflower, Willy cleared his throat. "Huey, Dewey, and Louie," he said. "Let's see, now. One of them had a red cap, one had a green cap, and one a blue cap, but I don't remember which one had which."

"I don't either," Margarite said. "They had a girl cousin, too. She had a pink bow. I forget her name."

"I don't know why everyone liked Mickey better than Donald," I said.

"Donald has a temper," Margarite explained. "That's why." She jerked her thumb at Willy. "Like him. That's why you liked *him*."

After we finished eating, we went back to Willy's. Margarite went in her room and closed the door.

"Would you like to call Hunter, or Alan?" Willy asked me.

Tears welled up. "I don't know," I said. "I don't know what. To say."

Willy shrugged. We were in his room, in front of his computer. He pulled up a list of phone numbers. He picked up the phone and listened for a minute and then put it down. He pulled up a mah jong screen. I leaned over to play and he started running his hands over my breasts.

"Stop it, Willy," I said.

"Oh, that's right," he said. "You don't want to do that."

"Right." I loved Willy very much now. There was a way I felt closer to him than to any other man in my life, but the chemistry that had made me run up the stairs to his room when I was sixteen to lie under a scratchy blanket with him for hours wasn't there any more. All of that sweetness — life had sanded it away.

He picked up the phone again and dialed a number. Alan said to come over. Margarite came out of her room.

"You're going to Jose's, is that right?" Willy asked her.

"We're just going to walk around," she said.

Willy and I drove out past Dominican College and up a winding street. Alan came out on the path and hugged me. Little sobs squeaked out of us and met somewhere above our heads. We went inside.

"Well, we'll still go on, won't we?" Alan had lived here over thirty years, but he still had the trace of an English accent.

"The man is dead," Willy said, gruffly.

"Well, no, it won't be the same, will it."

I sat in the middle of a long couch. Alan sat in a big wing chair on my left, Willy in a leather recliner on my right. It was a very nice house, with a lot of good stuff in it. It looked like the houses peoples' parents used to live in, in Palo Alto. I felt numb and disoriented.

"I have a little English stout," Alan said. "Would you like some? Some pot?"

He was being a good host, but I didn't want either of those things. Neither did Willy. Alan brought me a glass of water. Willy leaned back in his chair.

"Did you get a hearing aid yet?" Alan asked him.

Willy didn't answer.

"David X just got one, he was showing it off around the office," Alan said.

"They said I didn't need one," Willy growled. "I just have wall to wall wax in there."

Willy put his head down and dozed off. Alan showed me an album of photos of furniture he'd made. It was beautiful. Alan told me how big each piece was and how he'd made it, what kind of wood, the fun of solving different problems. We talked about writing. He'd written a little book, a history of a group of anarchists in Oregon. I told him I'd written a novel about the old days in Palo Alto, about the Love Scene, but it probably was different than the way he remembered it.

The night I graduated from high school Alan had been my date for the official party. He'd worn a fancy suit and I had a sexy party dress. We were high on Dexedrine, obnoxious and super-hip. I introduced him to my teachers as Oscar Wilde. We'd stayed less than an hour, then gone chasing the real party, from someone's rented room, to the coffee house, to the bookstore, to the Chateau. Some time in the early hours, just before dawn, in a caravan of three or four cars, we drove over the hills, up to Skyline and down through La Honda to the beach. There were fifteen or twenty of us. We sat on the ground in front of the general store in San Gregorio as the sun came up, waiting for the store to open so we could buy cigarettes. Jerry and Bob played and sang: *We're sailing down the river from Liverpool, heave away, Santy Anno ...*

I asked Alan if he remembered that.

"All those parties sort of blend together for me," he shrugged. "I don't think I could distinguish any one of them."

Willy woke up. It was time to go.

Alan looked at me. "Well, send me your stuff," he said. He smiled. "I'll be your agent. I know people — sixties people. People of our *ilk*."

This should have been good news to me, but I didn't even care. I managed a smile. "Thanks, Alan." He was just talking.

He clapped Willy lightly on the shoulder. "You're right, I suppose," he sighed. "It won't be the same."

"It won't be as good." I said. We all looked at each other, and then Willy and I left.

A lot of other people from the Love Scene checked out early. In a way, death and its romance had been as much a part of our scene as the love. Yet Jerry's death meant a little more; it was the end of something. There was more to miss than who he was, even more than who people thought he was, what they made of him. He radiated an orb around himself, like a sun, and wherever his music was playing I could step into that circle of sunlight and roses and meet heart to heart, like at a reunion, the people who had made my last months living at home so extraordinary: the Love Scene. Jerry and his music had kept my youth alive and told the whole world about it, and it came back for me every time I heard one of his songs from the speakers of a passing car or a boom box at the beach. In the early eighties, I'd been despondent and lonely at a retreat in the Catskills, miserable until I found a jukebox with "Shakedown Street" and "Staggerlee" on it. I played those songs over and over, remembering a love that was more an animating spirit than an obsession. The day after Jerry died , as I was walking home from the store I heard one of his songs pouring from an open window. *I don't know, it must have been the roses ...*

Once, Willy and I had loved each other with all the sweetness of the first pressing of jasmine flowers. As it turned out, we would always love each other in our own weird way, even when that fragrance was only something faintly remembered. Even when we were almost the only ones left.

International Operator

I've known Danny Amos for a long time, and his face holds a mother lode of remembered images for me: loud, smoky parties in railroad flats in New York and Berkeley, the steps of Low Library, crossing a corner of the campus in summer twilight arguing about books, or dreams. I remember him in a suit, best man when I married Paul in my mother's garden, signing the marriage certificate, toasting us in his singing Brooklyn voice. Now I know, because he's told me, how he was secretly amazed at our foolishness, which might have looked brave. Now, like everyone else we used to know — those who are still here — we've grown larger and grayer, like whales, telling our tales.

Danny remembers me studying Sanskrit with the television on. He asks how I could have possibly done that, and I tell him I was stoned. He wants to know how a Barnard girl could have turned out the way I did, and I try to explain — again — that I never was a real Barnard girl, I was always just an imposter from California. And he wants to know what that was like.

I didn't like the food in the dorms. I only ate lunch there when I was really broke. I preferred the Chock Full O' Nuts across the street, for a cream cheese sandwich on date-nut bread. This day, as I was coming out, I ran into Danny on Broadway. It was an October afternoon, my sophomore year. The sky was gray and heavy, more a preview of winter than a last gasp of summer.

Neither of us had a class that afternoon, so we went to the West End, and before long a couple of other guys we knew showed up and sat with us. I was drinking a Manhattan and the guys were drinking beer, except Danny. He had one in front of him, but he wasn't drinking it, just stirring it around with my swizzle stick, watching the bubbles.

I loved the West End, haunted by the shades of young Kerouac and Ginsberg. Late at night when it was crowded I liked to torment the bartenders by ordering complicated concoctions: stingers, sidecars, grasshoppers. This is what I loved: hoisting a glass. Drinking was like swallowing a shower of sparks, little lights that washed over and brightened my baseline state of anxious melancholy.

I'd wanted to stay in California after high school and keep on making the scene with my friends. But my mother insisted I go Back East. She wanted to get me away from bad beatnik influences, to become a young lady and marry a professional man. I'd kicked and screamed and finally, because I could not beat her in a fight, resigned myself to exile. I chose Barnard because New York City sounded better than the rest of Back East — and I could drink legally in New York at eighteen. I loved to drink and smoke pot and sleep with boys. I'd turned out just as boy-crazy as my mother said I would. Even Molly, my freshman year roommate, thought I was a little fast, just because I'd picked up a boy in the library once and gone back to his apartment to sleep with him.

Actually, I thought the boy thing was a little slow to get started here. East Coast boys were different from my California friends. There was something intense and furtive about them; they recoiled a little when I kissed them. They were broody and gray, like the weather, and they liked to talk about how much they hated their fathers. It took me a long time to stop pining for the bright sunlight pleasure of home.

Oh, I was miserable in those first fall shadows, and more so with the freezing winds of winter. In summer the Eastern trees were too bright a green, the air too thick and moist to breathe, the city grimy and dense, the sky broken into tiny irregular fragments. All I could think about was going back to California, sitting on the grass in my jeans and black turtleneck, singing with my guitar-playing friends, dancing and clapping to the beat of the drums and spoons, guzzling deep from the jug of bad red wine as it went around the circle. I knew I could get a better education on my own than I ever would in college. I would read books — poetry and philosophy — and have deep conversations with the people I met at coffee houses and bookstores and parties. I yearned for the dry fall hills that slowly turned green for the winter. More than anything, I missed the icy Pacific water turning my toes numb and blue until I ran back on the squeaky sand over the smelly, fly-speckled streamers of kelp. Here, there was no open sky — everything that should have looked open looked closed. Everything was too much used.

After a year, I had begun to get used to it. I was majoring in anthropology, though I had no interest in actually becoming an anthropologist. Going to the other side of the world and eating bugs and bats did not appeal to me; the adventures I wanted were of a different kind. I didn't really have any idea what I wanted to do after college. I was struggling too hard with each moment, too overwhelmed by the present to think much about the future. Anthropology was the best major; the required courses weren't too difficult and I could justify taking classes in just about anything that caught my fancy — linguistics, folklore, Sanskrit. Anthropology, after all, was the study of man, one of my favorite subjects.

But I didn't get used to dorm life, and it wasn't just the food I hated. I had never been with so many girls before, so exclusively with girls. There were social distinctions I wasn't used to: between

Jewish girls and not-Jewish girls, between girls from nearby and girls from far away, between girls who'd gone to boarding school and girls who'd gone to public school. There were girls who earned a little money by doing other girls' ironing and mending — for the girls who went away every weekend to Yale or Williams.

There was another girl from California in my class, from a famous rich family, that my mother had suggested I get to know. We were introduced, stared at each other for a few moments and never met again. Someone told me there was another beatnik girl, on the third floor. I went to investigate one evening and met a thin, sarcastic Negro from Cambridge who played blues guitar. We were too suspicious of each other to become friends, but I did buy pot from her a couple of times.

My roommate, Molly, was from Massachusetts and had gone to a fancy boarding school, but she was friendly, not stuck up. She was fun and a little wild. When I admired her pierced ears, she took me to a jewelry store in the East Eighties to get mine done. "It's like losing your virginity, isn't it?" she said.

Yes. My mother had told me not to, but I did anyway, and what could she do? We giggled. We tried to go to McSorley's Tavern to celebrate, but they didn't admit women and they wouldn't let us in.

Molly introduced me to some boys she knew. They were pretty screwed up, but so was I. They weren't really beat — they weren't as dirty and wild and poor as my friends at home. But they were smart and funny and tough in the New York way I was getting to like. We sat around in grubby, sparsely-furnished apartments listening to records, smoking pot, going on riffs that collapsed us into giggling fits. There were a couple of guys who played guitar and sang folk songs; and I taught them some of the songs we sang at home: *Santy Anno, Man of Constant Sorrow, Railroad Bill.*

Barnard students could take classes at Columbia College or the School of General Studies, and my new friends taught me how to make a class schedule: nothing before four in the afternoon, nothing above the second floor. I had been banished from my California paradise, but I was beginning to love New York. And by late November of my freshman year, I had a real boyfriend.

I had been checking my mailbox two or three times a day, hungry as a soldier for news from home. There might be a sad, sweet letter from my boyfriend, Party John, and some of the chicks wrote gossipy news: who broke up and who got together; who got married and who went to jail. Once in a while there was a sheet or two of notebook paper that had been passed around a table at Kepler's or St. Michael's Alley, a few words or a sketch from each person. And one day there was a postcard forwarded to me from the college registrar, from someone who knew only my first name and that I came from somewhere near Palo Alto. It was Paul, who Party John and I had picked up hitchhiking on El Camino, in the last weeks before I'd left. He was back in New York now and he was looking for me.

Paul was skinny and talked fast, and his straight, reddish brown hair flopped over his forehead into his green eyes. He seemed immeasurably sophisticated to me, a man of the world, an artist studying painting at Hunter College. On our first date, he took me to a café in Greenwich Village called Les Deux Magots and bought me a Jamaica Ginger Beer. He told me how he'd had to come back to New York when the Palo Alto cops picked him up as a runaway because he was only seventeen. They'd called his father and put him on a plane. Paul told me how much he hated his father, just like all the other boys I went out with. But he was nicer; that's what I told Molly. He was the nicest boy I'd met since I'd come to New York — and, after all, I had met him in Palo Alto.

The West End was a steamy, warm refuge. The drinks were making me feel loose and sparkly — I'd had a couple more. We were playing a game we played in bars and restaurants, moving the things on the table around as if they were chess pieces, clowning in our special off-beat intellectual way. Danny started a word game: think of words that end in -ic. I wasn't as worried about school as I should have been. I had my ways to keep worry away, even if they didn't always work.

Sometime in the middle of the afternoon, Dave Rosen came in and told us a U-2 spy plane had seen Russian missiles in Cuba, and Kennedy was threatening nuclear war if Khrushchev didn't take them out. There was a sudden frizzle of excitement in the booth. This could be the beginning of World War Three. We were all talking at once, asking questions. Danny's voice rose above the others for a moment, saying he had relatives in Australia and we should all go there.

Through my boozy fuzz, I was stunned. Russian missiles weren't the only thing in Cuba of interest to me. Right after Kennedy had been elected president, my father had started talking about moving to Cuba. He hated Kennedy; he didn't want to stay in the United States. His restlessness might have had nothing to do with the election — he might have been looking for meaning in his life. He might have just been bored with the suburbs, and wanted adventure and to be of use. He might have just been talking, but he wasn't, and sometime in the spring of 1961, just before I graduated from high school, he and my stepmother and their kids began to pack their things and distribute their furniture to their friends. My father gave me his big fur mittens from when he was stationed in Maine during the War, and he gave me back the ship-in-a-bottle I'd bought for him on Cape Cod when I was a little girl.

I felt a panicked sense of loss. I tried to talk with my father and stepmother about it, but they were offended that I didn't want to go with them. And I didn't want to go to a strange Communist country and live with my parents. I wanted to live wild and free, drink wine and take drugs and make love with everyone. It didn't seem to me like revolutionary Cuba would be the best place for that.

On a Sunday afternoon in August, just before I left for New York, my father and I sat in his car in the carport at my mother's house. It was just the two of us; my sister Annie must have been away at camp. Now my father and I, sharing a deep conviction that it was pointless to express feelings in a situation that would not change, looked skittishly at each other across the front seat.

"I'm not very good at goodbyes," he confessed.

"I hate them," I said, too quickly.

"Well, you've got to come and visit once we get settled."

"Sure," I nodded. My father never liked to see me cry. When I was very little, he'd teased me about saving my tears in a glass vial. He'd also told me to save them for "really important things," though he never suggested what those might be.

There was a brief, stiff hug, a kiss on the cheek, and I went inside. I was already packed for college.

Now, my father and his family had been living in Cuba for over a year. They wanted to stay forever. Every three or four months I got a mimeographed letter about their life in their luxury apartment on the beach in Vedado, taken over from some rich *gusanos* who'd moved to Miami. My father worked in the Ministry of Industry; his boss was Ché Guevara. The kids were in school. My stepmother worked as a translator. They had a maid. They were very happy. Everyone in Cuba was happy.

Across the booth from me in the West End, Herbie and Danny were having an intense conversation. Their heads — Herbie's curly, Danny's hair thinning even at twenty — were bent close together. I interrupted to tell them I needed to go to their apartment to call my father. It was a complicated thing, calling Cuba; I couldn't use the pay phone in the dorm. I had to place a call with the international operator and then wait for her to call back. It could be several hours, even a couple of days. Maybe even longer. I didn't try very often; it required a lot of planning, and then I had to find a place with a phone that I could sit and wait by. My father never called me. I don't know if it was because he couldn't get through the dorm switchboard or if he was just too busy working for the revolution and smoking cigars.

Our little group in the West End started getting up to go, scattering in the deepening afternoon. Herbie left first, to meet his girlfriend. Danny was still talking to some guy I didn't know, telling him he wanted to get to the bank to take all his money out. Nobody asked me about my father. They were too excited. They were too scared. I was scared, too. I knew the bomb shelter in the dorm basement offered no real protection. I knew it would be futile to cover my head and turn my eyes away from the blinding flash, as we had been taught in elementary school. I had read *Hiroshima* and *On The Beach;* seen photos of Japanese blast and burn victims, studied fallout maps. Palo Alto was a prime target, surrounded by defense plants. New York City would be a prime target too. If the Russians dropped an H-bomb here I would be vaporized, along with everybody else. And there wouldn't be just one bomb — the US and the USSR had hundreds, thousands of the things. Enough to turn the whole world into a cinder. It didn't matter whether Kennedy or Khrushchev pushed the button first.

Getting hung up about nuclear war was one thing; being

worried about my father was another. It went back a long way. When I was eight, my first boyfriend, Lance Borosov, took me to see *The Desert Fox*. I thought it was going to be an animal movie, but it was a World War Two story about Rommel. I should have known, since war was Lance's favorite thing. Most of the movie was boring, and I couldn't understand what was going on, but one scene transfixed me. It's when Rommel is executed for the plot to kill Hitler. He sits in a chair and the Nazis make him drink poison. For months after I saw the movie I had a recurring nightmare — it was my father sitting in Rommel's place, in the chair. This was in 1952, and everyone was talking about the Rosenbergs. They were a mother and father with two boys about my age, and the government said they were Communist spies. My parents and all their friends said they were innocent, but they got the electric chair anyway. My father was a Communist, and an electrical engineer, too — just like Julius Rosenberg.

"Danny," I said, touching his shoulder. "I have to call my father. Can I go to you guys' apartment?"

He gave me a puzzled look.

"I need to wait by the phone," I said. "I can't just call. He's in Cuba."

"Sure," he said. "Just go over. Tom's probably there, or Bob. I'll be home soon." He had his coat and scarf on.

"Wait," I said. "I'll walk out with you." I didn't want to be alone, even for a few minutes. I didn't like the idea of going to the apartment by myself, but I didn't want to follow Danny to the bank. I wanted to be with Paul, but he would still be at school.

Danny, Bob and Herbie shared, a huge, filthy apartment on 107th Street, between Amsterdam and Columbus. Right inside the doorway there was a hole in the wall that Dave Rosen had punched, when Molly wouldn't go out with him. It was a railroad flat on the third floor, six or seven rooms. You couldn't really count the kitchen as a room. Nobody used it. I looked in once; it looked like a garbage dump. Danny, Herbie and Bob actually lived there, but there were always at least two or three other people crashing. Someone was probably there now to let me in.

I walked back to the dorm and signed out for an overnight with my aunt. I didn't have an aunt, I'd invented one with Paul's phone number so I'd be there if anyone ever checked. I started walking down Broadway to 107th street. There was a cold wind blowing in from the Hudson. I was glad I'd had those drinks.

When I got to the apartment, Tom let me in. He wasn't a student, he just hung out with us and stayed in the apartment a lot. He wanted to be a writer. He told me he was pissed off because the world was ending before he would even be able to finish his novel, much less get it published. Once he let me in he went back to watching the news on TV. I went into one of the bedrooms that had an extension phone and dialed the international operator. I was starting to think the world *was* going to end and if it did I wanted to try to say goodbye to my father. Really, I wanted him to tell me it wasn't going to happen, that he was right there where the Russian missiles were supposed to be, and he knew. As soon as I'd put in the call to Cuba, I called Paul.

No one answered. He didn't have a phone in the room he rented but there was a pay phone in the hallway. His room was part of an old apartment in what had probably once been a good building, on the corner of Riverside Drive and 96th Street. The apartment had been divided up into separately rented rooms with a shared kitchen and bathroom. Paul's room was cluttered and overheated and it had a dirty window overlooking the Hudson and the Palisades. There was a big red neon sign across the river that blinked "Hellman's" all night.

The people in the other rooms were all crazy. Paul and I knew them all. The manager was a fat, Puerto Rican queer who wore housedresses and had pictures of wrestlers all over his walls. There was an old alcoholic violinist who was one of Mantovani's 101 strings. His favorite drink was a mixture of red wine, vodka and Tang, heavy on the vodka. I had one with him once or twice; it wasn't too bad. And there was a middle-aged Russian lady who wore a ton of bad makeup and spat "hoor" at me whenever she saw me.

I dialed the number again, and this time Dorothy, the English lady who talked to spirits through her radio, answered. I asked her to please write a note to Paul that I was at Danny's and put it under his door. She said she would, but she wasn't reliable. She might think a psychic message was enough.

I settled down to wait. Waiting for the Spanish-accented operator to call, waiting to hear my father's voice. Waiting for Paul. Waiting for men — something I already had some experience with. From the front room, I could hear the sound of the TV news. Tom was still watching. There was a book lying open on the bed — *Making It*, by Paul Goodman. It was a fat paperback and I figured it was either about sex or success; either way it would occupy me for a few hours. I couldn't concentrate on it, though, and pretty soon I fell asleep.

When I woke up, it was dark, and I called Paul's apartment again. He was home. Dorothy never gave him the message; he had been wondering where I was. He'd left two messages for me at the dorm. He wasn't sure if the world was going to end but he wanted us to be together just in case. I asked him to bring me a sandwich or something. I was hungry, but I didn't want to leave the apartment. The call from Cuba could come at any time.

When I knew Paul was on his way I felt a lot better. It was the same way I'd felt better about New York as soon as I'd met him. He'd shown me the city and introduced me to his high school friends from Bronx Science. He knew where to get pot and what the best radio stations were. He taught me how to ride the subways — to check the counters on the turnstiles and try to turn a zero, or a hundred, or a thousand; to ride in the front car and watch the lights. I was such a hick that he had to tell me the trains had drivers; I'd thought they were completely automatic, mindless missiles hurtling through the tunnels. We went to the Village and Grant's Tomb, and the Staten Island Ferry. From the outside deck on the last ferry of the night, Paul shouted out stanzas of Rimbaud in French. We'd come back to his impossibly dirty room and take Dexedrine and stay up all night in his narrow bed, listening to Symphony Sid and Jean Shepherd and making love, talking and talking and talking.

I wanted to tell my father about my new friends and my adventures — some of them, anyway. He'd lived in New York; maybe he had been to some of the same places. I never confided in my mother; I felt constrained by her worries and my fear of her, and I was glad she was far away. But my father had always seemed to support my explorations. At least, he was less definite in expressing ideas about who I should be or what I should become. I was not especially happy with who I was; I did not know what I was becoming. My mother accused me of not caring about my future, but it wasn't that I didn't care. It was more that I wanted a different future — someone else's future. I didn't know whose.

Paul got to the apartment just as Danny and Herbie came home. He brought two tuna sandwiches and a bag of potato chips, and Herbie had a pizza and some beer. Paul hugged me for a long time. They all wanted to watch the news so we went in the room where the TV was. Even when we moved all the junk off the couch, there wasn't enough room for everyone to sit there. Paul and I sat close together on the floor, leaning our backs against the couch. I saw a cockroach scuttle by but I didn't say anything.

When the phone rang, I ran back to the bedroom to answer it. There was the clipped voice of the international operator, alternating with the staticky Spanish of the Cuban operator.

And then my father's voice came crackling through. A moment later, my stepmother's, on an extension.

"Nonsense!" he shouted, when I asked him about the impending nuclear war. "There's going to be no such thing!"

He went on a little more about the *Yanqui imperialistas* and how they had learned their lesson at Playa Girón. Whenever my father spoke about the US, especially about Kennedy, there was a sarcastic sneer in his voice that I had heard a lot of, growing up.

"You ought to come down here and see for yourself," he said.

"Yes, come and visit us! We want to see you!" chirped my stepmother. They always talked on the phone together.

"I have school," I said weakly.

"School? This is more important than school!"

"I don't want to lose my passport," I said.

My stepmother wailed: "Oh!" That meant I had said a wrong thing.

"Nonsense!" My father was too genteel then to say "bullshit," the way we all would be saying in a few short years. "People come here all the time, lots of people. You won't lose your passport."

"Maybe in the summer," I said. I felt like I was starting to cry.

"Once you see what it's like here, you won't want to go back," he said. "It's a much healthier atmosphere."

I was somewhere else. "I was worried about you," I muttered, but he didn't hear me. Our connection was getting worse; the crackles louder than the words.

"Write to us!" My stepmother shrilled, and we all hung up.

I lay on the bed in despair. I could hear the muffled sounds of the other people in the apartment, talking and laughing over the distant dry television sound. I felt very alone, and after a little while I got up and went into the front room to find Paul. I sat down next to him on the floor. The news was over and they were watching a show about lawyers who help poor people. Paul put his arm around me and squeezed my shoulder.

Tom noticed me. "Hey," he said. "Your father lives in Cuba?"

"Yeah," I said.

"Wow, that's so cool, man — I got to go there. I hear it's amazing."

I didn't say anything, I leaned my head down against Paul's shoulder. I knew it made me mysterious to have a father in Cuba. It was a cool thing to have, like the beat-up leather bomber jacket Party John had given me. I still wore it; Paul had painted an expressionist eagle on the back. I put my hand on Paul's leg.

Without saying anything, we got up and went into the back room, the one I'd called from, and lay on the bed.

We made love hurriedly. I felt exposed, embarrassed by the close presence of the other people in the apartment. I couldn't stop thinking. I didn't come, but I didn't care. Squeezed together on the little bumpy bed, I didn't feel abandoned. I wasn't alone.

"Paul?"

"Hmmp. What?" He was falling asleep.

"Let's get married, so we can live together."

"Married?"

"Yeah, then I can move out of the dorms. We can get a place together. Downtown, where it's cheap. Near Chip and Marilyn."

Chip and Marilyn were two of Paul's friends from Bronx Science who'd gotten married when they were still in high school.

Paul snuggled me close and in a minute or so, he agreed with me, we'd get married. We were too tired to go back to his place, we just fell asleep where we were.

The next morning I had a Spanish class at ten. It was cold, starting to rain. Outside the bookstore at 116th and Broadway, Hubert the Yumpke Man was on his soapbox, waving his arms and shouting incoherently about "Columbumbia Uniperversity." The weather had driven away his usual audience, and the people walking by gave him no more than contemptuous smiles as they passed. There were a few dedicated students sitting at literature tables, holding umbrellas and coffee cups in their gloved hands. They had petitions and donation cans to support the student sit-ins in the South; James Meredith had just tried to enroll at the University of Mississippi. There was a table for the Fair Play For Cuba Committee, too. I walked past them, hurrying to class.

Downtown

Paul and I got married and moved to the Lower East Side. We were both nineteen. In '63 and '64 there weren't a lot of white bohemians living in that neighborhood. It was mostly old Ukrainians and a few old Jews and some younger Puerto Rican and black families and a few junkies and dealers. It was a poor neighborhood, with greasy aromas and immigrant shadows sealed in the walls of the old tenements, ghost languages in the streets. There were signs of an older time: free hard boiled eggs in the Ukrainian bars, and a synagogue that advertised a banquet room for Bar Mitzvahs, Social Events, Oufroufs. I couldn't find anyone who could tell me what an oufrouf was. The black and white and brown kids playing in the streets spoke their own dialect, a mixture of Spanish and English: *Abre el window, yo me voy al rufo.* Afro-Cuban music poured out of the buildings, but there was also a player of sad Jewish violin songs in Tompkins Square Park. It was a cultural rummage sale; I loved it.

Paul and I lived on the top floor of a six-floor walk-up on 8th Street near Avenue C. We had furniture and stuff from getting married — a hide-a-bed and an electric skillet. When we started decorating, Paul got ambitious and wanted to strip the walls to bare brick and redo the floors; I'd been with him to the loft where one of his art teachers lived, and it looked like that. But of course, we ran out of steam pretty quickly and never got past stripping one wall. Both of us had kind of short attention spans. Neither one of us was good at cleaning up, either, and we fought about that a lot. I had casual affairs, and he pretended not to care. We thought we were like a French movie, cool.

Then I met Alonzo, who was so beautiful it hurt me to look at him. It hurt, but I couldn't stop staring at that little guy: coppery brown, shiny and wiry. Walking down the street, he leap-frogged over fire hydrants. He had a face as sweet as candy, a sugar baby.

I met him one night when we were all sitting around in our friend Steve's apartment on East 2nd Street, me and Paul and a bunch of our other friends, smoking boo. Alonzo came in all sad because Gypsy, his pregnant girlfriend, had just left him and was living with somebody else. We knew them too; we all did dope together.

But I fell so suddenly and completely in love with Alonzo that night that when he got up to leave (I don't think he had a jacket, it was late spring and a warm night) I told Paul I was going out for cigarettes.

"Get me some too," he said.

I said, "Sure."

And I walked out with Alonzo like I was walking in my sleep. I walked with him to his place on Norfolk Street. It was a little studio apartment that Kenny Rubin's sister Barbara used to have. She'd painted it all black, just before her parents sent her to Central Islip, the loony bin. Alonzo had painted it over, light blue, but you could still see a little black coming through from underneath.

I walked up the four flights with him, holding his hand.

I stayed all night. In the very early morning, before it was light, I woke up a little, and Alonzo was covering me with a blanket. Paul was always grabbing all the covers off me. I fell more in love.

In the morning I had to go home and damn! I forgot Paul's cigarettes. We got into a fight. We fought all the time, but we were together. Neither one of us wanted to leave before the end of the movie. And Paul liked Alonzo too, everybody did. He didn't know how crazy I was about him.

I was in college, studying anthropology. Alonzo's mother was Cherokee; he told me Norman Rockwell had once used her as a model. His father was an Indian too, an Arawak, from a now-rare Caribbean tribe in Guyana. I knew Alonzo wasn't making this up — no one would make up an Arawak. Actually, I didn't care if he had made it up or not.

I was supposed to be working on a project for a primatology class, observing a group of langur monkeys in the Bronx Zoo. I got up early every morning, around nine, when Paul was still asleep. I grabbed my notebook, walked down Avenue C to Houston, but instead of taking the IND up to the Bronx, I went over to Rivington Street and down to Norfolk. Up those four flights. I woke Alonzo with a cup of sweet coffee, plenty of cream.

We played in his bed and then sometimes he played the guitar. He played classical music, like the Segovia records I'd listened to in high school. It was spring, and I'd bring strawberries, and a bottle of Beaujolais. We smoked some boo, if we had any. Sometimes I didn't go home until ten or eleven at night. Sometimes I stayed over.

And sometimes Gypsy, Alonzo's old girlfriend, came over too and we got to be pretty good friends. Beautiful Gypsy, with her big dark pool eyes and straight black hair falling over the angles of her pale face. I could tell Alonzo still loved her — loved her more than he loved me. I felt sad about it, but not angry at either one of them. She was carrying his baby, even if she was living with somebody else.

About in her seventh month she and the guy she was living with got married. He was Jewish, but they were married in a

Dutch Reformed Church, one of the more uptight Protestant denominations. The minister was annoyed that all of us — her friends — were there. It was just me and Paul, and Alonzo, and Steve and Dave and Benjy, but the minister seemed to think it should be a secret, shameful ceremony — in his office, instead of in the actual church. Gypsy wore a white maternity dress. She stuck out her big belly and laughed. She was happy; it was her wedding. Alonzo looked sad. I didn't know why she hadn't married him, but none of us ever talked about it.

After her baby was born and her mother moved down from Utica to help her, Gypsy and I started shooting dope together. The dope had sort of crept up on the scene gradually, like ink spreading in water. Gypsy's husband had been a junkie for years, but for years, he was the only junkie we knew. I don't know what changed. But one night Gypsy and I ganged up on Alonzo to turn us on. He couldn't stand up against the two of us, united, begging and cajoling and promising. Gypsy went first, then me. I saw tears in Alonzo's eyes as he slid the needle point tenderly into my vein. Right on the first try. I breathed all my troubles away and lay back. It was like being in perfectly warm water, inside and out.

One night a while after that Gypsy and I were both over at Alonzo's, all high and drinking wine. Alonzo and Gypsy kept looking at each other, and when he started playing with her long, bare toes, I left. I'd always known he loved her more, but still, I felt heartbroken.

I stopped going over to see him so much and started working harder in school. I started taking Sanskrit. By this time, Paul was using too, and pretty much everyone else we knew, too. Gypsy and her husband and baby and mother moved to Flatbush, and she had another baby. She'd stopped using heroin, but she was strung out on reds. Alonzo moved in with a woman named Penny who had a piano and a bad temper. I still went to see him once in a while there, on Avenue B, when Penny wasn't home. As he got more strung out he was less beautiful, like a tennis ball that had lost its bounce, but I didn't stop loving him.

Paul and I got money from our parents to live on, because we were in school, but we were spending more and more on dope. And more and more after a night class I was too loaded to take the subway and had to take a cab home all the way from uptown. Paul started going to the track with a friend of mine from Columbia who was good at math. They went to harness racing, which was crooked, so if you watched the tote board closely, you could see when the odds moved suddenly. That meant the big money, the smart money was coming in, and that would be the horse to bet. Paul brought home another two or three hundred a month with that system — that was a lot of extra money in 1964.

One night when Paul was out at the track and I was home doing my Sanskrit homework, Tony came over. He was a Puerto Rican guy from the neighborhood we bought dope from sometimes. He was always talking about how he wanted to be a pimp and have a lot of girls working for him, but to tell the truth he didn't seem smart enough to get that together. When he came to the door I told him Paul was at the track and I didn't have any money for anything.

Tony said, "That's OK, I'll give you a hit for free."

We sat at the kitchen table and I tied off with a little skinny dress belt I had, and he stuck the needle in and the curtain came down soft and warm and I felt good. Peaceful, like nothing could be hurtful or wrong.

I don't know how Tony was bothering me but he started making me nervous, so to get rid of him I told him I had to go out. I was just going to walk around the block but he came with me so I walked over to Steve's. There were a bunch of other people there and Tony came right in with me, smiling and talking to everybody, like he was everybody's friend. I went in the bathroom and threw up from the dope. Steve and the others were doing amyls but I didn't want any; I just smoked a little boo.

I lay down on a mattress. That was some strong stuff he gave me, Tony. I just lay out nodding and after a while they were all going out somewhere so I had to leave, too.

Tony was still there, and he said he'd better walk me home. I told him he didn't have to, but he kept saying it was dangerous and he wouldn't let me alone. I was hoping Paul would be home from the track by then, but they must have gone somewhere after because he wasn't. Tony came inside with me, right behind me. I was stoned and tired and starting to worry about the homework I hadn't finished. I told Tony he'd better leave, but when I lay on the bed he lay down next to me and started kissing me. I told him to stop but he lay on top of me and pulled my dress up. I didn't want this but I could feel he was stronger than me, and I was stoned. I figured I couldn't do anything about it anyway so I let him fuck me. I just hoped he'd be quick.

He humped and pumped and huffed and puffed and he was taking a long time.

"Oh God," I said, starting to cry, but he thought I meant I liked it. Then I heard steps, and the scratchy metal scrape of Paul's keys in the locks. Tony froze and his dick went limp and he said, "Oh look, now he's scared," and I pushed him away and pulled my dress down and got up.

Paul was in the kitchen and I ran over to him but Tony got there first.

He said, "I'm sorry man, I couldn't help it, she was all over me, she really wanted it," and I said, "No, Paul, it's not true," but he pushed me away and put his hand on Tony's shoulder and said, "Yeah, man, I know what she's like."

The next day I cut my morning class and went to see Alonzo. I told him what happened and he gave me a gravity knife he had. He told me: "When you cut somebody, go straight in their stomach, hard like a punch, and then go up." He showed me: Like this. He made me practice on him with the knife closed. I cried. I wanted to run away with him, leave Paul, but I didn't know if he really loved me. He seemed pretty happy where he was. I carried the knife in my purse all the time, but Tony took up with another girl we knew and he didn't bother me any more. I would never buy dope from him, either. By the end of the year I was hardly using at all.

Rumors of Death

Danny Amos called me this morning from Boston, where he lives now. It was the first I'd heard from him in months. I was depressed before he called, but he always cheers me up; that's been true for all the years I've known him, even though a lot of those years he's been pretty depressed himself. He called to say he'd sent me a note, which I hadn't gotten yet, and to say he'd seen my daughter in Boston and taken her to dinner and given her a present. It was her eighteenth birthday.

The day before she was born I was with Danny. We went to the zoo — Danny and my husband Peter and baby Josh and me and some friends of Danny's. Danny talks a lot about his friends and how important they are to him, and he is there for them — for us — in some deep unnameable way even though he's not always, in the present, the most responsive person in the world.

After we'd talked about my daughter for a few minutes he said, "Well, I have some bad news, but it's not about me and it's not about you. It's in the note, so I don't have to tell you about it now."

"Yes you do," I said. "What is it?"

He'd heard, in a peculiar way, that Kenny Rubin had died. I heard the part about Kenny being dead, but at first I didn't really hear the part about how Danny came to know that. I thought he hadn't known Kenny very well, and hadn't liked him at all. But I had met Kenny even before I knew Danny. He went to Cornell, where my first husband Paul had dropped out from just before I'd met him. The following year Kenny dropped out too and came down to New York. I'm not sure if he went to Columbia College, or General Studies — where the really cool people went — or if he just hung out with us. He was tall, and very skinny, even when everyone else was skinny, and he had thin hair and a small round face and wore rimless glasses. My friend Molly used to say he looked like a lentil.

Kenny wanted to write, or maybe he actually did write. For a while he had a job at the Brooklyn *Eagle*, where his mother worked. And then the *Eagle* folded and he went to Tangier. That was where we all wanted to go, like Burroughs and Kerouac. Danny told me, now, that someone else who knew Kenny had a theory that something really horrible had happened to him there, in North Africa, something that caused him to flip out.

"Of course," Danny said, "some people just said he was schizophrenic."

"I don't know what that means any more," I said. "I guess he was nuts, though."

When Kenny came back from Tangier, he moved in with a woman named Carol on East 10th Street. I was married to Paul by then and we lived just a few blocks away, so we saw each other a lot. Kenny had given up writing for painting big abstract canvases, and he was also painting his apartment in kind of a strange way. It was a typical Lower East Side place — two bedrooms and a big kitchen with a bathtub in it. Kenny was painting each wall a different color, and whenever he finished he'd start over again, repainting one wall at a time, each one another different color.

We all had a romantic view of insanity then; we thought of it as an art. And there was a lot of insanity around, too, only some of it from drugs. There was always someone we knew in Rockland, or Hillside, or Islip, or Bellevue. Carol had a fifteen-year-old sister who was living on the streets in the Village and the Lower East Side; their stepmother had been to see the same psychiatrist I was seeing, who — unprofessionally — asked me what I knew about the family. Kenny's sister Barbara had once stayed in a closet for ten days taking mescaline; when she finally came out she was talking gibberish. She lived on the Lower East Side too for a while, on Norfolk Street, in an apartment I moved into a few years later, after Alonzo had taken it over from her. She had painted all the walls there black.

I had a crush on Kenny. After Carol had moved out because she was tired of the paint fumes or Kenny's madness, I went over there once to sleep with him. The apartment smelled of paint. The sheets were grimy, but all the boys I knew then had grimy sheets. Kenny seemed very sad and distant. What did I want? I was married, but I slept with other guys sometimes. Paul said he didn't mind. We were trying to tell each other something, but we didn't know what it was.

Kenny was terribly skinny. A friend of Molly's and mine used to say her boyfriend was so thin that his bones poked her when they made love. I thought of that, lying with Kenny.

Afterwards he kissed my head. "That was OK," he said. "But something was missing."

"What?" My feelings were hurt, even though I didn't really disagree with him.

"I don't know," he said. "Joy."

I thought about that as I walked home on the midnight summer streets. Joy wasn't something I felt familiar with, even in sex. What made me feel worse than his saying that was that the next day he called up Paul and apologized to him for sleeping with me. That made me so mad that I never really talked to him again. By the time Paul and I were divorced, and a lot of other things had happened and I'd come home to California, I hadn't even seen Kenny for quite a few years.

Then, almost twenty years after I'd moved to San Francisco, he called me.

"Hello," he said. His voice had the same timbre, the same Brooklyn accent, as always, but it sounded a little mechanical. "This is Kenneth Barry Rubin. Have I reached the correct telephone answering set receiving number?" And then he read off my phone number.

"Sure," I said. "Hi, Kenny. How are you?"

His voice was friendly, but not warm. He sounded like a radio announcer. He interviewed me. He asked me where I lived: my address location number. He asked if I was married, my husband's name. If I had any children, their names and ages. He asked my occupation, my profession, how I earned my livelihood. He liked to use several different words for each question, as if he wanted to allow for many possible interpretations without losing any precision. He made me feel a little disoriented; he was so much crazier than I had remembered. But maybe I had remembered wrong.

We talked a little while longer. He had news about a lot of other people I hadn't seen or heard from since college. He had their address location numbers, in case I wanted to write. He told me he was well, although he seemed somehow to have become very large, or huge, or immense, or perhaps only wide around the middle. He had an ongoing legal situation with various government agencies; he was trying to get his records, he was engaged in litigation involving the Equal Opportunity Commission and the New York Housing Authority, among other government entities. He didn't provide me with the particulars. It had been a long ordeal, he said, but he was not giving up until he was satisfied, or vindicated.

He called every year or so. Sometimes more frequently, sometimes less. He always had the correct ages of my children and verified that the other information he had was still correct. He duly noted my latest divorce and expressed sadness that the marriage hadn't been successful. He remained the same; his legal dispute continued. He told me that his father "seemed to be no longer living, or perhaps had even died." I offered condolences, I asked after his mother.

I didn't remember his father, though I thought I might have met him once. I know I once met Kenny's mother. That was right after Barbara took the mescaline and stayed in the closet for ten days. When she came out she was so crazy that Kenny got scared and called their parents, who put her in a state mental hospital. I don't remember why Paul and I went with Kenny to his parents' house — maybe he was staying there, and we went there to see him. His mother — maybe with his father — came in later and sat down with us in the living room. She was bright and chirpy. Small, like Barbara. She explained that schizophrenia was caused by a chemical in the brain. She had worked for a newspaper; she had done her research. It had nothing to do with how the parents acted. Nothing. She repeated that, over and over, smiling at me and Paul and Kenny.

A few calls later Kenny had a new concern: It was about his sister, crazy Barbara, who had wanted to be a filmmaker and hung out with Jonas Mekas, whose short-shorn head was in a photo on the back cover of a Dylan album, who had painted her apartment black.

"There are rumors," Kenny said, in his nasal, mechanical voice, "there are rumors, which I have heard, concerning my sister, whom you may recall as Barbara, rumors that she may not be here any longer and may actually be somewhere else, and I can't reach her. But I don't know what to think."

Barbara appeared to have moved to Switzerland and borne several children, and now it was rumored that she had died in childbirth. Kenny didn't believe it, he was investigating, he was inquiring after her. He was concerned with discovering the truth of her whereabouts.

In the summer of 1962, the summer that Marilyn Monroe died, Barbara had been crashing at the same apartment that Paul and I were staying in, on East 6th Street. This was after the mescaline, but before the black apartment. She was dating a druggist and brought home huge plastic bags of pills every few days and dumped them out on the kitchen table. She also stole a good sweater of mine, dark green cashmere. I don't think I ever saw her again, after that summer.

But Danny told me later about how she fell in love with Allen Ginsberg. She hung out with him and Peter Orlovsky, and moved up to the country with them. She wanted to have Ginsberg's baby; she believed it would be some kind of magic genius. After trying to discourage her gently, Ginsberg became more emphatic and sent her away. Distraught and desperate, Barbara wandered through this small suburban town into a community of charismatic Hasidic Jews. A marriage was soon arranged for her, to a Belgian Jew, and she went with him to Switzerland. She had, indeed, died giving birth to her seventh child in eight years, in a remote Alpine village. I don't think Kenny ever accepted that.

But his information about other people we had known was accurate as far as I could tell, and I came to appreciate him. He kept track of dozens of us; he was better than an alumni directory. And then, there was that memory of him as he had been, and of myself as I had been, and of the times as they had been, that made me feel warm towards him and gave me the patience to listen and talk with him.

Somewhere through the years he'd been calling me, he'd given me a telephone answering set receiving number for Marty and Roberta, who I'd known in college and, in fact, introduced to each other. They were living in Marin, about twenty-five miles from me, and one day I called the number and we got together and got to know each other again. And it was, I think, through Kenny's interlocution that Paul got back in touch with me after many years of absence from my life, and we began to sort out some of the mess we had made with each other.

Kenny got a job with the 1990 census. I told him I thought it was the perfect job for him. He asked me who was currently residing in my household residence unit, and I told him that at the moment it was just me and my daughter; my son was in college in Los Angeles. I expected my daughter would probably be leaving home too, after she graduated from high school the following year. Kenny told me he lived alone, or by himself, in a self-contained dwelling unit. His household residence unit comprised one person: himself.

I imagined him sitting in a small, dark apartment in Jackson Heights. His hair had been thinning even in his twenties; it was probably all gone now. He didn't go out much. Too hot in the summer, too cold in the winter. And he might have been getting too big, perhaps bloated and pasty and shaky from medication. I pictured him with boxes of 3 by 5 cards; I didn't think he had a computer. He kept track of things the old-fashioned way, the way we had learned in college.

Then, he called several times within just a few months. He was concerned, perturbed, and he needed to know if I had heard of, or knew anything about, the Central Information Service, or perhaps it was called the Central Information Agency, or the

Central Bureau of Information. At first I just said no, I'd never heard of it. I tried to tell him not to worry, that no one would hurt him. But the seventh or eighth time he asked, in a moment of inspired frustration I burst out at him: "Kenny, *you're* the Central Information Agency! It's *you!*"

There was a silence at the other end of the line before he began talking of other things. He never mentioned the Central Information Office to me again.

It was only when Danny told me that Kenny was dead that I realized I hadn't heard from him in quite a while. When I called Marty and Roberta, I described the news as a rumor, the way Kenny had referred to his father's death, and his sister's. Did I imagine he had mentioned he was sick? It wasn't such a long time, was it? I had thought about him from time to time, but I hadn't really missed him. His name always came up when I got together with old friends.

Danny's letter came a few days later. It had been George Haywood who'd been the messenger of doom — Haywood, another skinny madman I'd gone out with a few times when I was twenty or twenty-two. He'd studied at the Art Students' League then, that's what I remembered, and now he'd come upon Danny in the Museum of Modern Art, accosting him like some disgusting ancient mariner. "Homeless and toothless," Danny described him. Haywood had shrieked out questions and lies and then advised him of Ken's death. His mouth, Danny said, flapped pink and wet like a sea creature.

I called Marty and Roberta again. I wasn't sure if they'd known Haywood; they hadn't known Danny very well.

"Haywood, sure, I remember him from high school," Marty said.

I told Marty how Danny had met him.

"God." Marty said.

And I told the rest of what had been in Danny's letter, the rest of what he'd found out. That Kenny's mother had said he had died of "natural causes." And that it had happened at least a year ago.

"It's hard to mourn someone who's been dead a year," Roberta said.

I wasn't sure I was finding it so hard. But then, I wasn't quite sure what I was mourning, either.

Marty had told me he'd seen him briefly, the last time he was in New York, and now I asked him, how fat had Kenny gotten, anyway?

"Oh, he was fat. But not *that* fat," Marty said. "I mean, not like he'd break a chair just by sitting down."

There was still some mystery. I wished I could remember whether Kenny had said anything about an illness, that last time I'd talked to him. But I didn't know if he'd said it, or if I'd only just now made it up. And Marty had told me something else about that last visit with Kenny. Marty hadn't had much time, so Kenny had come out to the airport to meet him, and just as Marty was about to get on the plane, Kenny had handed him one of those long, dense, handwritten-on-yellow-legal-paper *things,* one of those incoherent documents that crazy friends thrust on us from time to time. We're under no obligation to read them, but it is a kindness to receive them graciously.

Dare to Struggle

It was hot and dry. Peter said the air conditioning in the car gave him a headache and I had the window down only a couple of inches because I didn't want too much wind to blow on the baby in the back seat, finally asleep. The country music station from San Diego had faded out miles ago, and we'd forgotten to bring tapes, with all the stuff we had to remember for the baby. The desert stretched out before us on both sides of the road. It wasn't a real desert, like the Sahara or Arizona, with sand and cactus, it was just barren, flat land, an indistinct shade between gray and brown.

Nothing live grew here; it was desolate. The land was littered with little tumble-down houses and shacks and rusting cars. We passed a long-abandoned gas station with a peeling PEMEX sign. There was barely any traffic on the highway, but once in a while an old fifties car or a beat up pickup stuffed with an indeterminate number of people passed us going north. Imagining the lives of the people who lived here made me want to go home fast.

"It doesn't look like there's going to be any place to stop and get something to eat, do you think?"

That was Peter's reedy voice. He often sounded accommodating and tentative; he liked to ask "Do you think?" He'd been even softer when we were first going together: a gentle hippie pacifist living in a ghost of a timber town in the East Bay hills. We'd loved each other sweet and hard in his loft bed, everything smelling of wood smoke from the stove in the corner, with The Band playing

Music from Big Pink. For breakfast, Peter taught me to make seven-grain cereal, toasted first in an electric skillet. The electric skillet and a hot plate were all he had to cook on.

Now we'd been married for almost three years, and our son was nearly a year old. We ate supermarket food and lived in the City. We had bought a big house with a back yard in a nice neighborhood. Peter was teaching elementary school. I had everything I had longed for, for so many miserable years. I had everything I had cried for, but there was always something new to cry about.

I didn't say anything. I was hungry, but he was right, there wasn't going to be any place to stop until we got to San Felipe. I was picturing a *palapa* at the beach, like I'd been to on trips years before to the Mexican coast, a bar with tables out on the sand, a roof of thatched banana leaves, with cold Tecate beer and garlicky shrimp and a pile of fresh-made corn tortillas. A bowl of fresh, spicy salsa on the table. I could wait for that.

We'd flown to San Diego that morning and spent a couple of hours at the zoo before going south in this rented car. I was tired the way I'd felt tired since Josh was born, bone deep tired, spaced out, and quite possibly depressed. We would be in San Felipe in another couple of hours. We'd find the hotel and eat and I'd feed Josh and put him to bed. And then I could sleep.

"I'm all right," I said. "I can wait till we get there. Anyway, if we stop, Josh will wake up."

Something had happened to me after Josh was born. He was a big, round, curly-haired baby with a joyful laugh. I loved him madly; I could hardly take my eyes off him. But oh! the sound of the front door closing every morning when Peter went to work, and there I was, with the baby, alone. It was a fearful, acidy feeling, and it never really left me, even when I was obsessively shooting roll after roll of Josh-pictures, or sewing something for him on the machine, or standing in front of the refrigerator trying to decide what to make for dinner. Even when Peter came home, the feeling was still there. And he wasn't home more and more.

Peter took the car with him to work, but it wasn't a car I could drive anyway. It was a VW bus he'd bought when I totaled my car in a head-on on the freeway, the day of the first moon walk — a giant step for mankind. It was a great car, a red Valiant convertible, a hand-me-down from my mother. Dazed, I'd walked two miles home from the garage where the car had been towed. When Peter got home, he poured me a brandy and hugged me and told me how glad he was that I was all right. The next day he bought a new car that I couldn't drive. My legs were too short to reach the pedals. I told myself I'd learn the stick shift and get a cushion to put behind my back to move me forward. I thought I could make it work somehow, but something more than my beautiful little car had been smashed in that wreck. I wondered how much of the accident had been my fault, if I could really trust myself to drive. Especially after the baby — what if I got in an accident with Josh in the car?

I got used to not driving. What I didn't get used to was being alone and not alone at the same time. I was 26 years old but I thought I had already lived a very long time. When I'd dragged myself back to San Francisco, I'd wanted a writer's life, a scholar's life and — more than anything — a family. But like everything else I'd ever tried it had come out a little weird. I told myself the story of my life over and over again, like a rosary. I thought being married would mean not being alone. It had not yet sunk in, how alone you could be when you were with someone.

After Josh was born I was worried and afraid about everything. I was afraid Peter would only be a substitute teacher forever, that he'd never get a real job. I was afraid the old wiring in our house would catch fire and we wouldn't be able to get out in time. I was afraid Josh would die in a horrible freakish accident, like the baby next door who drowned one hot afternoon in a little plastic pool in their back yard. And I worried over Peter's obsession with politics and the Progressive Labor Party, even though I had introduced him to it in the first place.

Peter and I had met right after I'd come home to California to put myself back together after a bad time in New York. My mother — always nice to me when I was in serious trouble — helped me; I had a cute studio apartment in Bernal Heights and a great car, the car I later cracked up on the freeway. I had a good therapist, Dr. Jerry Berg. I was going to San Francisco State, taking courses as an unclassified graduate student, waiting to get into the creative writing program. I was going to find the right man this time, and have babies I could keep.

But whoops! It was 1968; there was that bad war. At school one day I ran into Dave Rosen, a friend from college. He told me about SDS and the Progressive Labor Party, and he talked me into going to the Oakland Induction Center for Stop the Draft Week. I started shaking when I heard the thunk of clubs on skulls, saw the blood-streaked faces, but the chanting and shouting and running made me feel alive. It was the first time in my life that people liked me when I was angry. And I had plenty to be angry about, my own hard times as much as the struggles of the Vietnamese people and their working class allies around the world. Even Dr. Jerry approved; I saw him at all the big demonstrations, marching along with the Psychotherapists for Peace.

I was in the right place at the right time; I was part of history. I wore a little red Chinese People's Liberation Army cap just like the girl in the Godard movie. Even though Progressive Labor wasn't the trendiest faction, or the one most of my old friends from high school were in, I liked those PL people then. They were tough and passionate, like the bad boys with greasy hair I'd loved when I was in junior high. I even thought it was cute that people who I knew had gone to Columbia and Harvard said "dese" and "dose." I liked the guys in their unfashionably short hair and blue work shirts, and the women in their braids and overalls. And we were women now, not "chicks." I waved my fist in the air and opened my throat to roar. I felt the wind of history lifting me off my feet. I was breathless at the microphone, talking to reporters. I was somebody — my picture was in the paper.

"Why?" Peter wanted to know why I didn't want to just spend time with him, going to movies and rock dances and out to dinner at new ethnic restaurants, normal things. Going to the country for the weekend. Visiting his friends.

"Don't you *care?*" I was astonished. "Don't you care about the war? You're a conscientious objector!"

He'd told me the whole story on one of those dark country nights in the cabin, how he'd lied to his draft board, told them he was a Zen Buddhist. He was from a small town and his family was important, so they gave him the 1-O.

"Well, of course," he said. "But you don't have to go to *meetings.* I mean, some people actually *like* to go to meetings. Let them do it."

I loved him, but I wasn't going to give up something that made me feel so good. I had become one of those people who liked to go to meetings. And what in the world could be more important than stopping the war? I tried to convince him that he was being selfish. He wavered. I gave the ultimatum: "Love me, love my dogma."

Peter came to a Mobilization with me, and the next week he

came to a meeting. He joined my PL study group. He, too, found a way to make sense out of his life. We became comrades, side by side at the barricades. I was proud of him, carrying the big red banner, holding up his end. *Dare to Struggle, Dare to Win.* I never dreamed my dogma would turn around and bite me.

At our wedding in the redwood grove in Golden Gate Park, we read an American Indian poem and a quotation from Mao. But already, I was tired of meetings that went on half the night and didn't resolve anything. I was sick of stupid arguments, and heartbroken from cutting off old friends because they didn't have the correct line on peace negotiations or cultural nationalism. The people I'd thought were so smart now seemed rigid and narrow-minded and bossy. When the Beatles recorded *Revolution* the Party issued an edict: throw out your Beatles records. Worst of all, they seemed to be wrecking the movement, not building it.

But now Peter was the one with an important role in the struggle, organizing substitutes into a radical caucus in the teacher's union. My sweet hippie boyfriend had discovered that he loved yelling at people. He was more enthusiastic and tireless than I had ever been, even with my little red hat. Watching him, I wondered if I had ever been that intense about anything, even about him.

The teeter-totter had tipped. He had taken my seat at the endless meetings I now begged off from. He spent more time on the telephone than I had as a thirteen-year-old girl. Every night he wasn't at a meeting, he brought new people home for dinner "to win them over." He expounded on the vanguard role of the radical caucus, the correct line between right-wing opportunism and left-wing sectarianism, the falling rate of profit. He didn't seem very interested in spending time with me or the baby. It seemed now he loved my dogma more than he loved me.

We had married on the winter solstice to avoid celebrating Christmas, a holiday we both professed to loathe — a commercial orgy of bourgeois materialism hiding in the wrappings of an oppressive superstition. It was Peter's school break, and we could celebrate our anniversaries with a vacation. And as much as he threw himself into his work, Peter was good at vacations. He'd grown up in a vacationing family, sailing in the summers, skiing in the winters.

I wanted to go somewhere warm and lie on a beach; I wanted to get away from everything. I wanted to go someplace without a phone, where Peter wouldn't bring those damned Progressive Labor newspapers. He was never without an armload of the things, peddling them even at my mother's parties. I didn't like to face it, but Peter had become a fanatic.

I had hopes for this vacation, fantasies of normal family life. Peter said he wanted us to "get closer," something he said more and more even as his other commitments took him farther away. I couldn't understand why, if he wanted to spend more time with me, he couldn't cut out one or two of the five meetings he went to every week, or a few of the Saturdays he spent selling his newspapers. I was beginning to realize that what he meant by "getting closer" was that I would get closer to him, not that he would get closer to me.

And all this talk about getting closer didn't fall out of the sky, as Mao would say. When Peter first wanted us to move in together, I asked him to come to therapy with me. I wanted Dr. Jerry's seal of approval, to be sure I wasn't making another terrible mistake. Peter was reasonable and sweet, but he didn't have much direction then. He didn't know what he wanted to do with his life. I thought Dr. Jerry could help him, and he did: within a month Peter had decided to become a teacher and was going back to school. By the time we were married, we were in Dr. Jerry's group for couples, learning how to communicate our needs and fight fair.

In couples' group we learned to negotiate everything, like the United Nations. We had official-looking contracts, written down on yellow legal pads and signed by both of us. This was meant to be an improvement over the secret, unspoken bargains of our earlier, more miserable relationships. Our financial contracts defined who paid how much for what. Our housework contracts specified how many hours per week each of us was to spend on each task. We took turns cooking dinner, though I noticed that on his nights to make dinner, he often just took something out of the freezer — something I'd cooked ahead. He never seemed to let any of our agreements interfere with what he wanted to do. And something deeper rankled: I wanted the sharing to come from feeling, not from a piece of paper. I wanted Peter to love me, and there wasn't any way to negotiate that.

We dropped out of the group a couple of months after Josh was born. Peter thought it was because the Party didn't really approve and it was getting more and more difficult for him to explain to his friends why we were going to a psychotherapist. I thought we stopped because with the baby and buying a house it was just too hard to find the time and money for it. We'd learned what we needed: we had the contracts, signed and kept in the filing cabinet with the rest of our important papers. And the most important agreement we had was that I would not interfere with his political work — I would welcome his friends and play hostess at his dinners for new recruits — on one diamond-hard condition: that he would never officially join the Party.

In my bones, I knew my queasiness over the Party wasn't the jealousy Peter accused me of. The longer we were married, especially after Josh was born, the more control I felt Peter had over me, and now the Party had more and more control over him. I was afraid if he actually joined, those other people — people that I hardly knew, people in New York I didn't know at all — would be controlling Peter's life completely, and through him, my life. And there was something else: I wanted him to do this one thing for me, just because it was important to me and because our marriage was important to him.

Finally, the shacks by the roadside were growing closer together. A hazy blue band of ocean appeared over the crest of a dune, and I saw it was no longer desert we were in, but beach. Hooray, vacation! I watched Peter driving. His beard was long gone, and his hair was short, so the people he was trying to organize wouldn't think he was a hippie and be turned off. I missed the beard. Of course I loved Peter, it was just that it was easier to remember that when I looked at the baby, sound asleep in his car seat in the back.

San Felipe had a large and expensive resort hotel, too bourgeois for us. We were staying, instead, at the "other" hotel, the one for Mexican tourists. It was a large, square, concrete-block building painted light blue inside and out. As we walked across the flagstone patio — a sleepy Josh in my arms, Peter dangling bags from his hands and shoulders — we had to step around piles of lumber and cinder blocks.

"Everything is OK," the proprietress assured us, smiling, leading. Our room was directly off the patio, a large room with two double beds in the center. I saw a dresser, a table, a wooden chair. But there was no crib.

Josh woke up, whimpering and pulling at his shirt. It was a thinly woven white cotton with a pale green stripe; I had sewed it myself from a remnant of curtain fabric. I hadn't used a pattern, only traced out a T-shape and doubled it. It was the way I used to make doll clothes when I was a little girl, dreaming of being grown up with my own husband, my own babies. I jiggled him in my arms, not sure where to put him down.

I turned to Peter. "I guess they don't have cribs here," I said. "We'll have to move one of these beds against the wall and pile pillows on it. It's going to be hard for him to sleep." Josh was used to sleeping in a crib or a playpen; he was conditioned to the sight of wooden bars. I would be waking up every hour or two to put him back to sleep. My head hurt just to think about it.

Peter frowned. "Oh, he'll sleep when he gets sleepy," he said.

"Yes, and he'll wake up when he wants to, too, and when he's hungry, and I'll have to get up and fix a bottle," I snapped.

"I could fix it," Peter muttered. He went out to bring the rest of our stuff from the car. I changed Josh's diaper and sat with him on the bed. I gave him a toy and a cracker and he sat contentedly next to me, smearing cracker goo on the bedspread.

To be fair, even when I'd been nursing, Peter had given Josh a bottle every day, filled with milk I pumped out of my breasts and saved in the refrigerator. He gave him the bottle in the late afternoon, when he got home from work. Before he went out to whatever meeting it was. I wanted to have a good time, relaxing at the beach with my husband and my baby, but I couldn't seem to get out from under the cloud of my unhappiness. In this shabby, vaguely dirty hotel room in Mexico, I felt like I was letting Peter down.

"I'm sorry," I said when he came back into the room. "I'm just so tired."

"Da!" Josh raised his arms to Peter, who picked him up and set him on the floor.

"Don't!" I said. "Put a blanket or something down first, it's dirty."

"Dih!" Josh said. "Da da!"

"I thought you might want a massage," Peter said. "I could sure use one."

But I was already picking up Josh and looking around for something to put him on. It was a lot more convenient taking care of him at home, with a playpen and a baby swing. I gave up and let him crawl on the floor. At the beach, he'd probably eat sand; there wasn't anything I could do about it. I didn't want to fight; I was tired and hungry. I didn't want a massage; even less did I feel like giving Peter one. "Let's go get dinner," I said.

When we went out, we saw there were no *palapas* along the beach. The only place we could find to eat was the fancy hotel. The fish was fresh, and the salsa was all right, but the tortillas seemed a little stale. There weren't any booster seats, so Peter and I took turns holding Josh. I fed him a jar of baby food and gave him pieces of tortilla to chew on.

It took a long time to get Josh to sleep in his strange, makeshift bed, but finally I put my pajamas on and lay down next to Peter in the other bed.

He reached out and fumbled with the buttons on my pajama top. I held his hands gently. When I was nursing, I couldn't stand to have him touch my breasts, and even though Josh had been weaned for a month, I still felt weird about it. I rolled on my side and kissed Peter's forehead.

"Goodnight, honey," I said.

I heard an unhappy sigh.

"What's wrong?" I had a pretty good idea.

He sighed. "Oh, I don't know ..."

The lights on the patio outside illuminated the room through the thin curtains. When I turned to Peter I could see his sneaky, sideways smile.

"I guess I kind of thought this trip would be a way to get closer together," he said sulkily.

"We *are* close," I said. I knew it was a lie, and that made me feel guilty. "Maybe tomorrow we could ask one of the women here to watch Josh for a while so we could be alone. We could ... take a nap, you know?"

There was that smirky smile again. "Well, yeah, but I meant more like, maybe we could have kind of an orgy or something."

I pulled back. "What, with Josh in the room?"

He shrugged. "I guess I didn't think about that."

I couldn't believe it. He hadn't thought about the baby? From my point of view, the baby was the whole thing.

Peter and I slept with our backs to each other on the saggy mattress. It was hard for me to keep from rolling into him. I didn't sleep much anyway; Josh woke every hour, crying because he didn't know where he was. An orgy. What was he thinking?

About the sixth or seventh time Josh woke up it was light outside and I thought about getting up. Josh was ready, waving and smiling. I thought Peter was pretending to be asleep. Why not? We were on vacation. There was nothing to do here except go to the beach, or maybe explore the village. I changed Josh and dressed him and put him on the bed with Peter. "Go wake up Daddy." Maybe I would feel better once we got to the beach. I had always loved the beach.

The ocean rolled in soft, gentle waves. Fishing boats bobbed on the horizon. The sand was coarse and a little dirty. Peter spread a blanket out and we put Josh in the middle, sitting up. I handed him a chain of big plastic beads that snapped together, and picked up my book. I was reading a Doris Lessing novel about being a young Communist in South Africa. Josh babbled and threw the beads down and set off crawling in the direction of the water.

"Could you watch him, please?" I asked Peter.

"I'm watching," he said. He picked up a file folder, some papers he'd brought.

He just didn't worry as much as I did, and there was nothing I could do to make him more like me.

While I was watching Josh play with the sand Peter told me that he had joined the Party. He said it in an off-hand, embarrassed way: "So, I guess I should tell you that I joined the Party."

"What?" I didn't mean, what did you say. It meant, what the hell am I supposed to do now? "When?"

"Oh, a couple of months ago," he said casually. He was smiling.

"That's not what we agreed," I said lamely.

Do you understand, Peter? Dr. Jerry would ask. Do you understand that she feels like you have a mistress, that she has to share you? That she needs more of you, that she wants you to limit your commitment? There was more to it than that, but Dr. Jerry's explanation made more sense than the truth, so I had let it go.

And Peter had agreed. Now he was telling me that he had done just what he wanted, agreement or no agreement.

Josh was shoving a fistful of sand into his mouth. I reached for him. My eyes were blurred with tears. My bluff was called, and I hadn't even known I was bluffing. I'd told Peter I'd divorce him if he joined, and now we would both know that I didn't want to be a divorced woman with a kid. I wanted another baby, actually, and I wanted to be married to Peter. Now I felt like I would still be married to him, but he wouldn't be married to me.

Josh was fussing, wriggling to get down. I held him tighter.

"Give him here." Peter held out his arms.

As soon as Peter held him, Josh stopped fussing. He loved

his Daddy. Peter lifted him to his shoulders and Josh laughed, clutching at Peter's hair.

"Don't you see?" Peter asked me, almost plaintive. "I want a better world for *all* the children."

It was what all the Progressive Labor parents said, when they picked up their kids at day care after having left them there for ten hours. I could even remember my father saying it to my mother.

In 1952, my parents had been divorced for a few months, and on Saturdays my father picked us up in his panel truck, me and my little sister Annie. We sat on sofa cushions piled in the back. That fall, there was an election for President. I was in third grade, and I went to a progressive Quaker school where most of the kids' families were for Stevenson. Two or three were for Eisenhower. When I asked my father who we were for, he said a name I'd never heard: Hallinan. He said it like I was dumb or crazy to ask such a silly question. It was obvious. Vincent Hallinan was the candidate of the Independent Progressive Party. He was running his campaign from jail, where he was serving a sentence for contempt of court. The person running for vice president with him was a Negro woman, Carlotta Bass. My father thought that was wonderful.

Saturdays and Sundays we drove around the suburban streets of Palo Alto in Daddy's truck, now decorated with banners and crepe paper and big pictures of Hallinan and Bass. Daddy's voice boomed through the speakers he had hooked up on top of the truck. He held the microphone as he drove. *Don't vote for Eisenson or Stevenhower, Tweedledum or Tweedledee. Vote for a real change — vote for Hallinan and Bass.*

I felt torn in half. I didn't want to hurt Daddy's feelings, but I hoped with all my heart that no one I knew would ever see me riding in that truck. I was mortified: why did my family have to be so weird? I was only eight years old, but I knew it was impossible for a Negro woman to be elected Vice President of the United States. When the kids at school argued about Stevenson and Eisenhower, I said I didn't care about elections.

Once, when I was pregnant with Josh, Peter got into a big fight with my father about Angela Davis. Progressive Labor had been started by people who quit the Communist Party because it wasn't radical enough, so Peter thought Angela Davis was a sell-out class traitor, and my father thought she was a revolutionary heroine. It was a stupid argument, and I could see a lifetime of stupid arguments rising in front of me, like grass growing higher and higher when nobody cuts it. I was so upset that I pulled Peter out into the hall and told him to stop it, please just stop it.

Now Peter was pretending to play with Josh but I knew he was really waiting for me to say something. He was daring me to say I would leave him, now that he had done what he had promised not to do, now that he had joined the Party. And what could I say? My heart was breaking, yet again. I would stay with him. I didn't want a divorce. I wanted Josh to live with his mommy and daddy, and I wanted to have that other baby that seemed already to be calling to me from another world. I wanted a regular family. But now I knew we would never do anything normal, like go to Europe, or to the symphony, or have a dinner party and talk about novels or movies. Peter would be embarrassing me for the rest of my life, getting into stupid arguments, carrying Party newspapers to sell wherever we went. My throat burned from not crying.

Josh was fussing, reaching for me again. I held him close. "He needs a bottle and a nap," I said.

We walked up the beach and across the road, back to the hotel. Peter had the room key. I fixed a bottle for Josh. The pediatrician said to give him nonfat milk, so we mixed it up from powder. I didn't measure, I just poured a good amount of powder in the bottle and added water from the big bottle of *agua purificado* that rested in a stand in the corner of the room. I sat on the bed and fed Josh.

The spring that Peter went back to school at Berkeley to get his teaching credential, there was a big demonstration in Sproul Plaza. I was at San Francisco State then, but I drove across the bridge in the red Valiant convertible. I parked somewhere and ran to the campus. There were thousands of people there: students, cops, curiosity seekers, old Berkeley radicals. And as I made my way through that mob to the steps of Sproul Hall, suddenly there was Peter's sweet face before me, beaming in the nest of his wiry red-brown beard and long hair, his eyes smiling behind his metal-rim glasses. I was wearing my Chinese army cap, my hair pulled back, no earrings, ready for battle. What a miracle to find each other in that throng! We fell together, laughing, on fire with the joy of the struggle, of ourselves. What had happened? Who had changed? I wanted it to be like it was, but I didn't want to be who I had been.

In the pale blue room, in the Mexican hotel, Josh looked at me with an expression that seemed full of concern, like he wanted me to feel better, but I knew he was just intent on his bottle. Sometimes the milk powder didn't quite dissolve and clogged the nipple. I wondered if that might be happening now, but he was still sucking.

Peter was sitting in the leather armchair, writing on a yellow legal pad. He looked pleased with himself, and relieved. In a flash I saw that he had had a plan, maybe one of his Party friends had suggested it. He would take me on a vacation to a place that I liked, we would eat in restaurants and sleep in a hotel. His wild, ardent lovemaking would convince me beyond any doubt that I needed him, couldn't live without him. His passion would be contagious — more important, his passion for the class struggle would infect me, and I would embrace the revolution as I embraced him. After all, it had worked before, when he had followed me.

Well, his plan hadn't worked out exactly — he'd forgotten about the baby. But it didn't matter. He had only misjudged the basis for my dependency, not the extent of it. I was despondent, but it was just no big deal for him, now that he could see I wasn't really going to leave him.

High on the window, a big wasp was buzzing and whirring, beating itself against the glass. I was too afraid of being stung to get up and open the window to shoo it out. Peter was busy writing something — a lesson plan, or a leaflet. He was busy working; he didn't even notice.

Beautiful Clothes

Susan forgot her baby at a party once, but we all argue about where it happened. Susan doesn't like to talk about it. My sister Annie says it was at her house. I say it was our mother's house, at Annie's wedding. I remember it so clearly, Susan and Michael coming back to my mother's front door about a half hour after they left. And Susan so embarrassed, saying: We forgot our baby! Susan doesn't deny that it happened, but she always turns it into a story about how badly my mother always treated her. In fact, she says it couldn't possibly have been at Annie's wedding, because my mother told her she couldn't bring the baby.

My mother had a real animosity toward her, it's true. She never liked women who were too beautiful or too successful, and Susan was both. But the thing my mother always focused on was Susan's leaving her baby behind. No one — except Susan — ever mentioned that Michael had left the baby, too. And they came back; the baby was sleeping in the middle of my mother's bed (at least that's what I remember) with pillows piled around her so she wouldn't roll onto the floor. She was fine.

I've given up arguing with Annie about whose house it was, where the baby was left. She is so sure she is right. I never thought to ask my mother, and she's gone now. Her memory predeceased her by several years, so even if I'd thought of asking I'm not sure it would have helped. Annie was a closer friend of Susan's than I was then, in the late sixties, when Susan and Michael first moved to San Francisco. Annie was married to a wacko and Susan was married to a wacko, and the husbands were best friends. Susan's wacko was much more successful that my sister's wacko, even then. It was a big-dog, little-dog buddy thing.

Susan and Michael lived in a big, sunny flat near Coit tower. Everything was pretty and modern and matching, like in a magazine. All Marimekko and clean windows, with views of the sparkly white and rose city. They gave a big party in the spring and served May wine in a crystal bowl, with strawberries frozen in the ice cubes. Susan pointed out the famous writers and musicians who were there. "Gee," Annie said brightly. "It's too bad John and Yoko couldn't make it."

Susan's baby had the most adorable baby outfits. Susan and Michael worshiped her. I didn't know then how unhappy Susan was — she was so pretty and smart, and she had such beautiful clothes. She worked at a hip radical magazine while Michael stayed home with the baby; she was getting famous for her feminist essays. But maybe I did know she wasn't happy. She looked a little sad one day when I visited her, sitting on the carpet in that beautiful apartment, nursing the baby and smoking. Cigarette ashes drifted gently down over the baby like gray snowflakes.

I didn't go over there often. We weren't very good friends then. Her radical politics were not the same as mine; we were in different factions. And she was too chic, too straight for me. I'd carried that impression from the very first time I'd seen her, years before, when she'd flown like a bright, raucous bird into my Lower East Side tenement apartment, when I was married to Paul. Our friend Danny Amos brought her over; showing her off. They didn't stay long; we were all going out in different directions.

Only after she and Michael had broken up and she'd moved to a cottage in Berkeley with her daughter did we begin to get closer.

She came to visit in the new house Peter and I had bought. She'd stopped working for the magazine and had a contract to write a book. She was collecting things from the flea market, buying and selling. She brought me a beautiful white silk shawl with delicate embroidery. I cooked a fancy party dinner. She put her little girl to sleep on a folded quilt in the corner of the dining room. She was tender; she didn't forget her.

And then I went to see her in Berkeley. Her cottage was behind a big brown-shingle arts-and-crafts house, at the end of a walkway. It reminded me a little of the witch's house in Hansel and Gretel.

"That looks good on you," she said. I was wearing a blue sweater. It wasn't anything special, but Susan knew all about clothes. Everything she wore was beautiful; she could bring style to a pair of jeans and a t-shirt.

She reached out and fussed with my sleeves, unrolling them and folding up the cuffs. She straightened my collar and pushed me to a mirror. "Look!"

She was right, of course, it looked better. Then she showed me the dollhouse she was making for her daughter, exquisitely decorated with fancy papers, fabrics, tiny things. She was writing a book about sex; she was interviewing all her women friends. We lay on her day bed, smoking pot and talking. She said mean but clever things about a man we had both slept with, and I couldn't stop laughing.

The next time I came she gave me a big bag of her old clothes — a fashion care package. I was grateful for her hand-me-downs. I hated to shop for clothes. If you asked me, I didn't even know what size I wore. I'd buy something because I liked the color or the feel of the fabric. It never occurred to me to look at the fit of the shoulders or where a hemline hit my leg. Susan shook her head. "I'll help you," she said.

When Peter came into my hospital room a few hours after our daughter was born, I was spilling over with gratitude and love for him. Such a beautiful baby, other-worldly, still faintly bluish, with long dark hair. Her shoulders were covered with a fine dark fuzz, like an exotic forest creature. A peaceful baby, waking with small, sweet noises instead of insistent wails.

But in the months that followed Nina's birth, our marriage cracked open, like ice in the spring. Deep fissures split an already crazed surface. We were on completely different tracks, speaking only the minimum we needed for household logistics. He was out almost every night with his Party comrades, and I wondered if there was a particular woman he was spending time with. I knew we were moving away from each other, but I didn't seem to be able to do anything about it. I couldn't make him love me, or want to stay. I withdrew into my head, my babies, my friends.

Susan had met a rock and roll drummer and moved to his house in Fairfax. He had been in a famous band. That was Susan's style — she always did the most famous thing, the most important thing. Now she was more glamorous than ever. Her interviews with celebrities appeared in national magazines. We didn't see each other often, but that didn't surprise me: she had that exciting work, and a new boyfriend. Still, one day in the early spring, she called and asked me to come visit her in her new house.

Going to Berkeley from San Francisco had been an ordinary, gritty drive, but going to Marin was like crossing into Wonderland: the Golden Gate bridge rising red out of wisps of fog, a glance back at the sparkling city, then through the rainbow-painted tunnel into the green hills. I got lost looking for her house and had to stop and call for directions. It was the drummer who answered and told me how to get there.

And then I found it; halfway up a hill behind the Deer Park at the top of a long, steep flight of stairs: a modern house of redwood and glass. It was a little before ten in the morning. I'd come over straight from dropping Josh off at nursery school. I carried Nina and a diaper bag up the stairs. The door was open, and I stepped over the threshold into gypsy fairyland.

A jungle of plants hung from the ceiling and in the windows. Sunlight lit the green leaves and the bright colors of fabrics, pictures, multi-colored objects lying everywhere. Susan's decor was dazzling and funky at the same time. It reminded me of the pair of jeans I'd embroidered in seventh grade, a brief fad at my school in the late fifties, a harbinger of hippie things to come. I had decorated mine with bright flowers and leaves and teenage words: Cool. Zorch. Crazy. I wondered if Susan had done that too. I could feel our likeness — I thought she, too, must have pored over the notions counter at Woolworth's when she was a little girl, spending her allowance on bright colored thread and buttons.

Beyond the big front room, Susan was sitting in the kitchen with a cup of coffee.

"Hi," I called. "I got here."

She didn't answer. She didn't seem really awake yet. She was wearing a long cotton t-shirt dress, navy blue with a small white pattern. It was just a housedress, maybe even a nightie, but she looked beautiful in it. Her daughter stood next to her, crying that she wanted Susan to take her to school. Susan ignored her and rolled her eyes at me.

"Do you want coffee?" she asked.

The little girl kept on crying.

"No, thanks," I said.

"I'll take you!" Susan stood up, turned to the child. "I'll take you, I'll take you, just a minute, just wait a goddamn fucking minute, will you?"

She walked back into another room — her bedroom. Her daughter didn't follow her, she just stood in the middle of the kitchen, dressed for school, whining louder now:

"Mommmmmy! Take me to school!"

I sat down at the table, holding Nina. Susan stayed in her room for about ten minutes and the whole time, her daughter didn't stop. And then she came out, and we all went together, down that long flight of stairs. We piled into Susan's car and took the girl to her school.

I didn't figure it out right away, but Susan had gone back to her room to sniff a couple of lines of heroin. I'm not sure how long she'd been using — it was kind of a fad in Berkeley at that time, so she might have started there. Or maybe it was the drummer. And not the next time I came over, but maybe the time after, I did a line with her. And later, a couple of times, I bought a dime bag from her to take home, where it would last me about a month. She shorted me, too, but I didn't mind. I bought that blue t-shirt dress from her, too. I used to wear it all the time, with a coral necklace.

I don't know exactly when I realized I was in love with her. After all, I had known her for more than ten years, and she wasn't even my closest friend. But this wasn't about being best friends, it had all the crazy, stupid earmarks of love. She was beautiful, her dark shiny hair hanging to her shoulders; she was slim, tanned all over. It was beginning to be hard for me not to gaze at her; she was making a spell. I made my pilgrimage to the fairy palace two, three, four times a week.

Usually I brought Nina with me; Susan liked to hold her. We drank coffee, sunbathed naked on the deck, complained about men. She was still collecting things from flea markets. Her gypsy tent was filled with quilts, shawls, dresses, bits and scraps of velvet, fur, silk, calico. She offered me clothes she didn't want anymore, but now she wanted me to pay for them. And I did. I was completely enchanted.

Peter's rich uncle died and left him a lot of money. It was an embarrassment to him; he didn't want it. I protested when he started to give it all to the Party, and, grumbling, he gave half to me. I bought myself a brand new car to drive back and forth over the Golden Gate Bridge, a light blue Mazda with a rotary engine. I loved my new car, it was part of the princess magic of visiting Susan. And when she cried because her old car had broken down, I gave her my old but serviceable Rambler.

"You *gave* it to her?" Peter asked. "You didn't get anything for it?"

I shook my head. It wasn't the money he cared about. He'd never liked Susan.

"It's my car," I said. "She needed it, and I gave it to her. I thought you were a communist."

Susan and the drummer had become involved in something called The School. It was something mysterious; she didn't talk about it very much. But one time when I was complaining about Peter, she told me I should do a "training." It sounded religious and weird, not like anything I wanted to do. I couldn't even imagine how Peter would react. The last thing I needed was something else to fight with him about.

"It's not a religion." Susan looked at me, deep black eyes. "You should do it," she repeated. "You'd see everything differently. You'd find out who you are." But she still wouldn't say what it was.

Whatever it was, it didn't seem to be making her happy. She was always crying now. One day she cut off her hair, her almost-black hair that had hung straight to her shoulders. She sat at her kitchen table, looking into a hand mirror.

"Why did I do this?" she asked me. Silent rivers creased her cheeks. She would not be comforted. The drummer had another girlfriend. She had another boyfriend. Once he came over when I was there, a large, loud man. I didn't like him.

A few weeks later, when I drove up to the house I saw the Rambler parked in front, gutted and burned out. She told me Rocky — the side boyfriend — had set it on fire by accident. I liked the drummer. I didn't understand why she needed another boyfriend, especially one who was stupid and mean. I might have been jealous, I suppose. That day she told me she and the drummer were going to New York together, to do a special advanced training with The School.

And while I was missing her and sulking, sniffing the last line of the dime bag I'd bought from her weeks ago, Peter left me. I didn't expect that, even though by that time we were hardly talking to each other. I never thought he would actually leave. But he did, and there I was with the two babies, miserable with failure and loss. I took the kids to my mother's for a couple of weeks. Now I was always crying, too.

As soon as I heard Susan was back from New York I raced across the bridge to see her. I was alone; Peter had taken the kids East to visit his parents. She looked more beautiful than ever, glowing as if the summer sun was emanating from somewhere inside of her. The drummer wasn't home and there was a beautiful man in her bed: delicate, androgynous, smelling of sandalwood oil, a turquoise earring gorgeous against his olive skin. He seemed to be not even human, but something Susan had made from patchwork and beads. She introduced me: his name was Morningstar.

The light streamed into the living room. A huge string-of-pearls plant hung from the ceiling. Susan put on a Steely Dan album and the two of them, slim and nude and tanned, led me in the series of calisthenics people in The School began each day with.

When we finished I was stoned out of my mind. I guess it might have been the breathing. We drank coffee and hung out for a little while. I didn't say much. All they talked about was The School and they used words I didn't understand. Then Susan said she had to go somewhere, and as if she were loaning me one of her dresses, she told me to take Morningstar back to the City with me.

He stayed for two or three days, sleeping in my bed. There was an intensity about him, a way that he seemed to look at me with such total attention that I almost thought he could read my mind. He made love to me once, on the second day, after I'd been stewing and worrying about why he didn't like me. I felt as if I were falling in love with him, and when he was gone, I went crying to Susan.

"Just let him go," she said. "He's not worth it."

"But why do I feel this way?" I sobbed.

"He's like a thirty-second hit at the flea market, you know? You see something that's so beautiful, you just have to have it, but when you get it home — ehn? It's not even pretty. Just forget about him."

She'd become so wise, I thought. Maybe I did need The School. I called and signed up for the next program. Maybe I'd meet someone there — someone like Morningstar. I wanted to glow like him. Like Susan. I wanted to do whatever she did. I wasn't envious of her. I didn't want her life — she was always so unhappy, sitting at her kitchen table, weeping. No. I just wanted to breathe her in, to absorb her.

As powerful as my attraction was, she was a moving target. Just as I imagined us growing closer, intertwining our lives, both of us in The School on our journey to enlightenment, Susan told me she and the drummer were moving to New York. She gave me some of her clothes and her string-of-pearls plant. I hung the plant over my bed.

In New York, she and the drummer worked for The School, then broke up. She was getting deeper into heroin, but I didn't know that for a couple of years. I got more involved with The School myself, and then I got married again. I ran out of money and had to get a job. I had the kids, I had a life. I still thought about Susan a lot. I still loved her. Every so often she called, usually very late at night — it would have been even later in New York.

She cried on the phone. "Help me!" she sobbed and hiccupped. "Please help me. I'm so fucked up." But she was so far away. I didn't know what to do.

We had only slept together a few times, but the frightening intimacy of loving her body stayed with me, indelible and immediate as my own skin. All the time she was gone, even when I was married, and after, I longed for her — all that time when she was traveling on a dark highway in a scary foreign country.

I didn't see her again for several years. There were those phone calls, and a few letters in her round scrawl. And then The School announced a two-week summer program in the Catskills. My husband didn't want to go, and he didn't want me to go, either — he didn't like me to get too far out of his sight. But I had to go. Peter would take the kids, and I got an extra part-time job to earn enough money for the plane fare and tuition. I would borrow a tent and bring a sleeping bag to save the cost of a room.

The thought of seeing Susan again was my secret beacon. But she wasn't there! And the program itself felt repetitious and empty; there was none of the ecstatic glow I'd always felt in the meditations. Other people formed little cliques with their friends in neighboring cottages or on the same floor in the large hotel. I didn't know any of the other people who were camping. A woman in the tent next to mine woke every morning with loud groans and complaints.

I was not a very skillful camper, and I had forgotten how hostile the East Coast countryside felt to me. It rained a lot. I was uncomfortable and, within a few days, sick. At every meal in the dining room, throughout the day at the big tent where the program sessions were held, my eyes scoured the grounds for Susan's form, my ears tuned for rumors of her arrival. She would come, she had to. I had to see her.

One afternoon a harsh shout came across the lawn from an unrecognizable figure: "You didn't even recognize me, you bitch!"

She was right, I hadn't. She was puffy with extra weight, maybe forty pounds. Her hair was graying, stringy; her skin dull and yellowish. She was there for only for a few hours, to sell dope. I wasn't buying, and she had no time for me.

When the training ended I stayed in New York for a few days. I was depressed, becoming disillusioned with The School. I dialed Susan's number over and over, listening to the ringing, ringing, ringing. When I finally reached her she told me to come to her apartment. It was near where I was staying, on the Upper West Side.

She had moved to this apartment over a year before, but there was almost nothing in it — just cardboard boxes, still unpacked, and a few crappy sticks of furniture. We sat together on a dirty sofa. I asked about her daughter; she was staying with Susan's parents. I sniffed a line of heroin with her, but it didn't make me feel good, only dull and tired. We hardly touched. She had to go out, she said. I knew why. I walked back to where I was staying and lay down and waited for the dope to wear off. It was the last time I ever did any.

But we weren't over yet. That happened much later, after she had gotten clean and moved back to Oakland. There had been years when she was in and out of jail and rehab and back on the streets. She phoned me a couple of times a year from that life in the underworld of New York and Minneapolis. It was like hearing a voice from the moon, so distant. She reminded me of the Dylan song we all used to listen to so much: *Once upon a time you dressed so fine, threw the bums a dime, in your prime — didn't you? People said beware doll, you're bound to fall, you thought they was all kiddin' you … How does it feel? To be on your own?*

Yes, she was a rolling stone, with no direction home. What had that moment felt like for her, when she knew she had turned the corner and was caught, the quicksand up to her chest and rising? There is something spellbinding in the horror of those moments: when you realize you've lost control on a curve of road, or that your teetering marriage has irreversibly begun to fall off the cliff. Like the sudden comprehension in the moment after your foot slips — the flight! and then you know you can't stop falling.

A year after I left The School, after that training in the Catskills, I was divorced again. My life had completely changed, once more. I wasn't seeking God any longer, I was finding. I had a whole constellation of spiritual friends and guides — Sufis, Buddhists, non-denominational mystics. Nearly every evening I was at a class or meeting, guzzling down Divine love and wisdom like soda pop.

I was on a retreat in the New Mexico mountains above Taos when I got a letter from Susan's sister Amy. They had done a family intervention. Susan was in another rehab program, and Amy thought this one was going to work. I rejoiced, I prayed, I went to healing circles. I bought a small teddy bear I carried with me to ceremonies and sacred places. When the bear had been passed around many circles and a multitude of holy people had added blessings and prayers, I mailed it to her at her rehab center in Boston. I imagined that after she healed she would come and live with me, that we would go Sufi dancing together and sit in my garden drinking tea and making fun of the men we had known.

But when she first came back to Oakland, to her new clean and sober life, she told me she didn't think we should have sex any more. She was right, it was too complicated. We were better off just being friends. And we were good friends, talking on the phone nearly every day, going to movies and restaurants together, hanging out. She came to a couple of Grateful Dead shows with me; we bought Guatemalan pants in the parking lot. During the intermission she found a twelve-step group that met in a hallway under a bouquet of yellow balloons. When her memoir of addiction and recovery came out I sat next to her at her book party. And she still gave me beautiful clothes. Once she called me at work from a nearby radio station where she was being interviewed about her book. I ran out to meet her on the sidewalk and she handed me a silk blouse, printed in tones of gray, black and red. "For work," she explained. We hugged tight.

But over her years of drug dependence I had forgotten how independent she was. We loved each other, but we had a hard time striking a balance. We were both older sisters, and it was maddening when we tried to boss each other around. She had stayed with The School; I had new teachers. She asked me if I'd heard a new album she liked, but I was more interested in classical music. I thought she sometimes had tacky taste in books, and we didn't like the same movies, either.

We were beginning to separate. I took up gardening, she took up knitting and birdwatching. I didn't like her boyfriends, hunky dumb guys she pushed around. When I saw her with her polished, brittle women friends from The School I saw her as she had been in those first San Francisco years: not the woman I loved, just someone in a magazine. Glossy and superficial.

Why do people fall out of love? We had both changed a lot, but not in any really deep or important way. We'd always argued, about fine points of left politics, about feminism, about people we knew. We didn't like the same men, but that was probably a good thing, as she'd once pointed out. She was notorious among some of my other friends as a boyfriend-stealer. It wasn't any of that. It was just that she didn't sparkle for me any more. She just seemed more like everybody else.

My mother began to decline, not very gracefully. I complained about her weird phone calls, her drinking, her demands. Susan was not sympathetic — it was the old antagonism.

"Oh, your mother." she said. "Your mother wouldn't let me bring my baby to Annie's wedding."

I thought it had been at Annie's wedding party that she left her baby behind, but I didn't want to bring that up. I had a friend I couldn't talk to about a big painful thing in my life. I had to draw a box around my mother: don't try to talk to Susan about this.

We never had a big fight, like breaking up with a man. We never told each other we wished we'd never met, or that we'd wrecked each other's lives. That would have meant both of us admitting how much we loved each other, and then, each of us would have had to encounter within ourselves the particular ways we drove each other crazy. We just saw less and less of each other.

We emailed Jewish jokes. She said the telephone made her tired; I said, me too. We would always be in touch, always care for each other, but now we stayed at a little distance.

I would be wearing her beautiful clothes for years: silks and cashmeres, a beautifully cut jacket, a hand-painted velvet top. They always made me feel glamorous, I never worried that they might not be in style. And without knowing it, she'd given me something else: the gift of understanding why it was I was such a fool for a certain kind of love, a love for people who weren't really there. Because they didn't demand that I really be there, either.

We are both more present now when we see each other those few times a year. We go to lunch, and afterwards she often wants to shop a little. I never do, but I go with her into the shops, and as she fingers blouses and sweaters I hang back like a sulky child. Then I remember. We go back a long way. She'll go home soon.

Not Like Most Women

"I want to pluck your eyebrows," Amy said.

"Don't be crazy."

"Please?"

Amy was like that. She'd ask if she could squeeze a blackhead, or want me to squeeze one of hers. I didn't get it. That kind of thing was over the line for me, too intimate, even for a lover. I could pluck my own eyebrows. I used to, anyway, when I thought it was important.

Eyebrows weren't quite as bad as blackheads.

"OK," I said.

Amy told me to lie on the floor on my back. We were in the living room, where there was a thick shag carpet and the light was still pretty good in the afternoon. She got tweezers and the paper of cocaine we had. She rubbed some on my eyebrows.

"Wait," I said, sitting up. "Let's do a couple of lines first."

I could still feel the pinch of the tweezers, but it didn't bother me. Amy was really concentrating. When the phone rang she let the machine pick it up.

"I wish I had a boyfriend," she was saying.

Amy said that all the time. She had two songs: I-wish-I-had-a-boyfriend, and I-wish-I-could-lose-some-of-this-weight. She was in love with a gay guy who was very sick. Not AIDS, this was before AIDS, in the seventies. He had Hodgkin's disease, though, and he was probably dying. She went to see him almost every day, and he was teaching her sign language. He wasn't deaf, but he had a lot of deaf gay friends. Amy wanted to learn sign language because she thought it would be helpful some day. She was the kind of person who saved up helpful things, waiting to use them. Not like her sister, Susan, who was always looking for help.

The person who called hung up on the machine. I thought it was probably Ray; he never left a message. He was paranoid about answering machines.

Ray was my boyfriend. I had a boyfriend, and I only weighed 105 pounds. I already had what Amy wanted. Maybe that was why she was plucking my eyebrows. Maybe it was some magic ritual thing she was doing, and when she was finished I'd weigh 20 pounds more and she'd weigh 20 pounds less, and she'd have Ray.

Amy was my roommate. She'd originally come to the West Coast to see her sister Susan, but when Susan had moved back to New York a year ago, Amy moved in with me. She helped me take care of my kids — I had a four-year-old son and a two-year-old daughter. Right now they were with their father for three weeks, visiting his parents on a lake in the midwest. That's why Amy and I could lie around on the floor and do coke like this.

There was a familiar echo in our living situation. Ten years before this, I'd lived in New York with Leah — Susan and Amy's other sister — and helped take care of her three-year-old daughter. Even though I had some heavy things going on in my life at the time, it was a happy arrangement. Leah and I were so tuned in to each other that we not only stopped at the grocery store on the same day but forgot the same things. We each had a few boyfriends, passing them back and forth like sweaters.

I wouldn't have minded sharing Ray with Amy, but she was afraid of him. She was afraid of men; that's why she didn't have a boyfriend. The only one she wasn't afraid of was gay and dying.

Amy wiped off the mirror and handed it to me. Still lying on my back, I looked at my face. She sat back on her heels.

"Don't you love it?"

I wanted to make her happy. "Yes," I said. My eyes looked larger and farther apart. I looked more awake; I guessed that was good. I wondered if Ray would notice.

Ray had a wife, that was the only problem. Not the only problem, but the biggest problem. His wife knew he was seeing me, and she knew my phone number. He'd probably given it to her; married people are like that. Pauline would call and scream at me when Ray was with me. I'd hand him the phone and she'd scream at him. Even if he just hung up, even if I hung up as soon as I heard her voice, she had an effect. It was like she had teleported herself and was standing in my bedroom, screaming.

Amy poured the rest of the coke out on the mirror and chopped it into lines. We each did a couple of fat ones. The coke made me hot for Ray; I hoped he was coming over later. With all the problems in the relationship, it was the best sex I'd ever had in my life — hallucinatory sex. Transcendental sex. Sex that made me feel like my teeth were on fire.

Amy was wired. She put on her sweater and picked up her purse from the hall table. I watched her. I didn't really see why she wanted to lose weight; I thought her body was adorable — curvy and soft.

"I'm going to see Michael," she said. "I'm probably going to Berkeley after." She put her purse on her shoulder and shaped her hands into a figure she waved towards me.

"What's that mean?" I asked.

"I love you," she said, and went out the door.

My nose was running and I was starting to come down from the coke. I didn't want any more; besides, it was all gone. I missed my children. I wanted them to come home so I could lead my normal life again, running around like a monkey trying to take care of them. I wanted to forget about all this other junk. I went upstairs and ran a bath. I looked in the mirror. My eyebrows looked terrific.

While I was in the tub Ray called.

"Come over," I said.

"Oh, baby," he said. "You know I want to."

That meant no, but I held out hope. "Well, why don't you, then?"

"'Cause Pauline went out, and I have to babysit."

I didn't know why men always called taking care of their kids "babysitting," but I decided not to bring that up.

"Why don't you bring her here?" I said. Meaning the baby. "She can sleep in the kids' room."

When Ray had first started coming over, he used to bring his daughter. It probably had to do with some lie he was telling his wife. And then, he thought that somehow his baby would play with my kids, and we could play with each other while the kids were playing. But of course they were much too young, it was horrible. It was the only thing Ray and I ever even started to fight about, what to do with the kids. Now mine were gone, swimming and making sand castles. Getting red as lobsters because nobody would remember the sunscreen. When they grew up, they'd get skin cancer and everyone would blame me. I was the mother, I was supposed to be responsible.

Ray was explaining that he couldn't bring the baby over to my house with him because Pauline had taken the car, too, and the baby's carseat was in it, so even if I drove to Woodacre to pick him up — which I wasn't offering to do — it wouldn't work. Lately he always seemed to be explaining why something wouldn't work, usually meaning he couldn't see me, but he kept calling me and acting like he wanted to.

"Hang on a minute," I told him.

I set the phone down on the bathroom floor and got out of the tub. I pulled the plug from the drain. I wrapped a towel around me and took the phone into my bedroom and sat on the bed.

"I really want you, Ray," I said.

Really, what I wanted was Amy. I wanted Ray and Amy both together, and another gram of coke and maybe some Cuervo Gold to take the edge off.

I was dreaming. Amy would freak if I ever so much as mentioned it as a fantasy.

"She's supposed to be home by eleven," Ray was saying. He was whining a little. "She went to a lingerie party."

While we were talking on the phone, I was trying to decide whether to paint my toenails. Amy had each of hers painted a different color. My favorite was a deep violet.

Ray had a few strange ideas about health and beauty. For instance, he told me to always keep my nails clipped short, so I wouldn't get karma in my hands. I didn't know what interesting objection he would have to toenail polish but he probably had one.

A good thing about Ray was that he never minded if the conversation stopped for a while. He was willing to hang out.

"What's a lingerie party?" Finally I asked him.

"Oh you know," he said. "Like Tupperware, all the ladies get together at somebody's house, only it's all sexy underwear and nighties, that kind of stuff. Love oil."

"Oh." It wasn't anything I was very interested in. "Do you like that kind of stuff?" I was thinking if I could get him turned on over the phone, he might figure out a way to come over.

"Not really," he said. "But, you know, she needs to get out some. With the baby and all."

And all your running around, I thought, but I didn't want to start feeling sorry for Ray's wife. I felt sorry enough for myself. I was skinny, but I wasn't happy.

"Come over later if you want," I said. "I'm not going anywhere."

Everything was quiet again. Oh God, I thought. I hope he comes over.

"I'll see ya, babe," he said.

When he said that, the way he said it, I knew he wouldn't come over, and he didn't, but I didn't let myself wait on him, either. I smoked some hash I found wrapped in a piece of foil in my jewelry box. I found some gray capsules there too; I thought they might be MDA but I couldn't remember. I didn't take any but I didn't throw them out, either. I thought I'd ask Ray if he knew what they were when I saw him again. If I saw him again.

On Sunday, I talked to my kids on the phone.

"We went in the lake," said my baby girl.

"That's nice, honey. Was the water cold?"

"Very freezing cold!" she said.

It made me sad, that I wasn't there. Sad that I wasn't the one to wrap her towel around her and rub her warm while she shivered and shrieked.

Her brother took the phone. "Hi, Mom! Bill took me out on the boat." Bill was his grandfather, a retired surgeon who sailed and played golf. Josh had called his grandparents by their first names since he'd first started talking — no Grandpa this or Granny that, just Bill and Jane. They tried to correct him but it didn't make any difference. He was a sweet boy, but very stubborn about what he wanted to call things.

After they hung up I went into the kitchen.

Amy was at the stove, stirring something. She was making vegetable soup. She'd made a pot of coffee in the Chemex, too. I poured myself a cup and stirred in a teaspoon of powdered ginseng and about as much honey. It was the way Ray drank it. It tasted weird and a little gritty, but it was a nice peppy hit and I needed it, down as I was from missing my kids.

I was watching Amy cook and something about the shape of her back reminded me of her sister, Leah. They didn't look all that much alike, but there was a family resemblance. They had the same hair: straight, coarse, black. The kind that would start to go gray early. Leah was four years older than Amy; I wondered if she was getting gray yet. I hadn't seen her since I'd left New York.

When I'd first gotten to be friends with Leah, we lived around the corner from each other, near Grand Street on the Lower East Side. I was living with my boyfriend and not getting along with him. I had a part-time job running a mail-order psychedelic poster business for a hippie psychologist who hung out with Timothy Leary. I hardly ever saw him, but I had a huge crush on him. The poster business was in his apartment on Avenue A, but he was gone most of the time, in the country with Leary and some other famous psychedelic people and the artists who actually made the posters. I never did anything about my crush on him; I was too intimidated.

Leah and I moved in together when we broke up with our boyfriends. They'd both been bad boyfriends — mine hit, and hers was a junkie. I was pregnant. I babysat Leah's daughter in exchange for her paying the rent on the apartment. We lived together like a happy family; we liked hanging out together. She played the guitar and we sang English ballads together.

Leah worked in a Japanese import store and dated a Japanese guy she'd met there. She fixed me up with his friend, a poet from Hokkaido, who took me out to nice dinners. He liked elegant Chinese restaurants, or Beefeater martinis and steaks at Max's Kansas City. We talked about poetry, and about the Ainu, the indigenous people of Hokkaido. Even when I started to show, he never asked me about being pregnant. He never made a pass at me, either. After a couple of months he went back to Japan.

When Urban Renewal drove us from our happy home, Leah wanted us to find another place together. But I wanted the bonus money I could get from the city if I moved out of New York. I was tired of it anyway. After my baby was born, and the tearful taxi ride with my mother, after I signed the papers giving him up, I was ready to go home to California. I needed to mend.

On a sticky summer night, Leah and I were talking while I packed boxes. One of the neighbor guys came over to have a beer and congratulate us on the Six-Day War, just over. "You Jews can sure fight!" he said. Leah and I laughed, but then she went in her room and closed her door.

When the neighbor guy left, I put a Jefferson Airplane record on and packed books. About eleven, we were out of beer and I decided to go up to the Old Reliable, this bar on 3rd Street we used to go to. I knocked on Leah's door but she didn't answer. I figured she had gone to sleep.

But when I came home from the Reliable, for some reason that I can't remember now I went in Leah's room, and there was something funny about how she was sleeping, and then I saw her empty tranquilizer bottle on the floor. I was just glad her daughter was staying with her parents for the weekend; I called for an ambulance and then I had to call them.

Leah had her stomach pumped at Bellevue and then she was all right, but things weren't the same between us. I left for California about a week later. I gave her all my furniture instead of selling it to her like I had planned. I bought her daughter a stuffed horse.

After I moved, we wrote a few letters and called each other once in a while, but it was hard to stay in touch. She married a guy she met in her new building and had another baby. I guess she was happy. Neither of us ever mentioned what happened just before I left.

Watching Amy stir the soup, hearing her humming, made me think about all of that. I didn't like Amy's soups so much; she put in too many different things. I liked soup better with just one or two vegetables, but Amy cleaned out the refrigerator drawer and threw everything in there. Leah had been the better cook.

Amy took a cup of coffee and sat down across from me. She drank hers black, without the ginseng.

"I talked to my parents last night," she said. "They want me to move back to New York."

"Well, that's nothing new," I said. Her parents didn't like her so far away. Her father, in particular, had opinions about California. He didn't think it was quite a real place, a place he could imagine anyone seriously wanting to live. About once a week, he and Amy's mother told her she should come home.

She looked nervous, sipping coffee. "Yeah, but, I'm moving back. In September."

"Well, great," I got up from the table. My stomach was fluttering. What could I say? She could do whatever she wanted, but I was kind of pissed. I didn't like changes in my life that I had no control over. I was going to miss her. And now I had to find a new roommate and a new babysitter. My kids liked her, too.

But of course when I thought about it, I could see why. She wasn't happy; nothing was happening for her here. Her boyfriend wasn't even really a boyfriend, and besides he was probably going to die soon.

Amy's eyes looked worried. "You can keep the piano if you want," she said. "It's only fifteen dollars a month."

She had just started renting the piano a couple of months ago. She was going to teach me how to play. I tried to put a good face on it. "No, really, Amy," I said. "I think it sounds great for you. Maybe you'll meet somebody there, fall in love."

A few days later, the day before the kids were coming home, Ray and I were lying in bed. We'd just made love, the first time all week. It was great, too. He'd made me tell him what I wanted to do with Amy, and he was so psychic it was as if he could actually conjure her, make her be there. And then he'd made me feel like we were out on a very thin transparent platform in space, weightless. Like the only thing that was keeping me from flying away forever was a fine, strong silk thread, and he held the other end. After, he rolled on his side, leaning on his elbow, and touched my face with his other hand. His dark brown curls were damp on his neck.

"Babe, you are the sweetest thing," he said.

I felt like a cat in the sun.

"I wish I could just stay here with you," he said.

"Yes," I purred. "Me too."

He sighed and sat up on the edge of the bed, reached for his jeans on the floor.

"Where you going?" I asked.

He put his pants on and sat back down on the bed. "Gotta

go," he said. He stroked my back.

I kept my eyes closed. Inside me was a little girl who wanted to scream and fall on the floor and hold on to his legs and wail: No, no, don't leave me. Baby, baby, please don't go. But I would never let that girl out of the box.

I opened my eyes and smiled at him.

"Well," I said. "If you gotta go, you gotta go."

He leaned over and kissed me.

"What I like about you, babe," he said. "You're a free spirit, you don't hang on. Most women — "

"Oh, shut up," I said. "Don't tell me about most women." I turned my face down into the bed. I wasn't going to ask him when he was coming back, either. I turned back and watched him go, and only after I heard his car start did I remember that I'd forgotten to ask him about those gray capsules. I should just throw them out.

Lost Boys

"I've been watching you for fifteen minutes."

How could I fall for a line like that? Here's how: he looked good. A long mop of curls fell over his forehead, like the "waterfall" hairdos of the bad boys I loved in eighth grade. He had a nice smile for me, too. Fog from a disco machine drifted around the room. He was sitting on the floor, one leg tucked under him and the other extended straight in front. An elaborately carved walking stick lay beside him. I thought it was a prop, an affectation, but it didn't bother me.

It wasn't exactly a costume party, but some people were oddly dressed. A middle-aged man was in a suit jacket, business shirt and tie and nothing at all below the waist. But even though it was a noisy, theatrical party, it probably would have been dull if everybody hadn't been so stoned. I had taken a little acid — a hundred mics, just enough for a buzz. Someone was passing around a pipe filled with ibogaine, an African herb that made you feel perfectly still and quiet inside, like a mountain.

I smiled back at the good looking man on the floor and floated away into the smoke and fog. There was music and I wanted to dance. I did love to dance. I was a dancing fool, putting on music when I woke up in the morning and dancing around the room. I danced holding babies, I danced by myself. At parties and clubs I even danced to that terrible disco music they played then, in the late seventies.

Out of the corner of my eye I was watching that man, and when he got up to get a drink, I saw his stick wasn't an affectation, it was something he needed. He walked with a lopsided, swinging gait that looked more like dancing than like being crippled.

I'd come to the party with Nora, my roommate. She'd been living in my house for a few months. She didn't have a job and she was broke, so she didn't pay any rent. Instead, she babysat and started little decorating projects which she didn't finish. Some of my furniture was half-stripped, and the new slipcovers on the couch were still unhemmed. She sometimes made elegant little meals for us. We liked her very much, me and the kids.

We were all in The School, a mystical-human potential group where we did complicated meditations and exercises and went on weird diets. It was all supposed to lead to enlightenment. I didn't really believe it, but the first program of doing those exercises intensely for several weeks had brought my mind to a state of relaxed clarity that was new, and amazing. I'd met some exciting people. Everyone in The School seemed to have a bright, shiny look. Gazing deeply into each other's eyes and telling our nastiest secrets had scared some people away, but those of us who stayed could feel very close to each other very quickly, even if we didn't really have much in common or even like each other very much.

I found Nora in an armchair, draped over a skinny, young English guy. She glanced over at the man I was pointing to and told me his name was Bobby. He was a writer; she'd known him in New York.

Someone put on a new Rolling Stones album, very loud. Unwinding herself from the English guy, Nora got up and grabbed my hand to dance.

As we spun around together, she leaned close to shout in my ear over the music.

"I think we should take Bobby home."

That sounded fine to me. Nora and I weren't exactly lovers, but we sometimes took a man or two to bed with both of us. When she had someone over and I didn't, she worried I might feel lonely or jealous. She almost always knocked on my door: "Want to come play with us?" Sometimes I did, sometimes I didn't.

But just as we were ready to leave the party, she changed her mind, and went home with a girlfriend, so I had Bobby to myself.

I told Nora the next afternoon, when she came home. "It was pretty good. But I wouldn't want him to be the only person I slept with for the rest of my life."

She had a way of laughing that I was never sure about. Never sure if she was laughing at me, or why. Usually I just laughed along with her, but this time it irritated me.

A few days later, there was Bobby at my door, carrying a guitar. We sat on the couch and he sang love songs and sad songs: Eagles, Jackson Browne, that kind of thing. I'd never listened much to that music, so I didn't know most of the songs. Before I found out whose they were, I kind of assumed they were his own creations. He played well and he had a nice voice. He told me he'd played in a bar band in the Virgin Islands. We smoked a lot of pot; he'd brought some, and then I got out some Colombian I had.

After a while he put the guitar down and told me he'd been thinking about moving to San Francisco. He'd been staying with some friends in Stinson Beach. He could see I had a big house, and I told him he could move in here if he wanted. The kids shared a room, and I had a room, and Nora had a room, but there was still another bedroom that I sometimes rented to people from The School who were traveling through. I liked having a lot of people around the house, it made me feel less isolated and crazy than when I was just living with my kids.

I had been in The School for about two years then. All that meditation had left a pale yellow light in my head and I was in a mildly psychedelic state most of the time, which I sometimes enhanced with substances — as commonplace as coffee, as exotic as yage, and everything in between. Everything in the physical world seemed alive, like it had when I was a little girl: the arrangement of dinner plates set on the table looking like a face; the windows smiled. The trees weren't just moving passively in the wind but waving a personal greeting to me. I had become a little psychic, I could seep right through my skin into a man's body. It made for great sex, experiencing both people's ecstasy. And now here was Bobby, back at my door with a smile and a bag of good pot in his pocket. He didn't bring much with him when he moved in. The guitar, a footlocker full of t-shirts and jeans, a typewriter. He also had a prescription for Percodan and a set of red satin sheets.

"Who is that kid?" Josh asked me at breakfast, the first morning he'd seen Bobby in my bed.

"That's not a kid," I said. "That's a man. That's my friend Bobby. He lives here now."

Josh was six then, a wise child who sometimes saw things more clearly than I did. I'd always thought I was looking for a strongman, a protector. I didn't know how much my heart was longing for a boy.

I was just a little too old to have been a full-out hippie. In the Summer of Love I'd been serious and political, and then I'd married Peter and had babies. I felt like I'd missed out on an extended childhood, and Bobby gave that to me. With Nora, we lived together like teenagers whose parents had left them alone while they went on vacation; we filled our shopping cart with

Oreos and frozen pizza and pot pies. I had some money from my divorce; Bobby still had some of his book advance. We were carefree as puppies.

Josh and Nina warmed right up to him. He was clever and funny in a dark, New York way, like my friend Susan. He was romantic, too, courting me with flowers and songs like a troubadour. Love might have snuck up on me, but I was already half-blind, primed by a lifetime craving for a love that would, as Rumi puts it, "turn all the dirt in this world to shiny gold." The School had tuned my nervous system to a fine, fevered pitch and made my flesh feel translucent. And of course there had been a man to show me how to work all that: Ray, who I'd driven to the airport for the last time only weeks before. That wildman psychic bodyworker had cracked me open like a crab, and Bobby was the lucky recipient. I was splayed out for his pickings. We had sex every day, every night, a lot of it.

My doctor had taken me off the pill a year before and put a tiny copper thing in my womb, shaped like a lucky seven. I wasn't supposed to be able to feel it, but it was subtly irritating, and I was hearing from other women that these things weren't healthy. I was too spoiled now for the icky, inconvenient ritual of diaphragm and goo. When I saw the doctor next, I made an appointment to have my tubes tied.

I was supposed to be at the hospital at eight in the morning, but at seven, I called to cancel. The doctor didn't seem annoyed, or even surprised. People must change their minds all the time. Even though I had two beautiful children and didn't need any more, when I looked at Bobby's green eyes and tight dark curls and thought about how clever he was, and how musical, I wondered. In a passionate moment or two I might have thought: oh, I want your baby!

But Bobby told me he was sterile, because of his accident. When he was nineteen, his friend had taken a curve too fast and flipped the car, and Bobby broke his back. The Accident had happened, by coincidence, just two weeks after I'd given birth to the baby I'd never held, the child whose name I didn't know. It was as if Bobby and I shared some terribly unfortunate star, and we had now been given to each other to heal.

But how was he sterile? Even people in wheelchairs have children. Bobby was vague, as he usually was about medical things. He didn't like to talk about it. It didn't quite make sense to me, but then, when I was with Bobby, I didn't care about sense. Reason was the enemy. I thought all my suffering had been caused by thinking too much. Meditation quieted the constant yammering of the inner voice, but it wasn't enough. I had always longed to be loved so hard, to love so much that my mind left me. And it seemed at last that I'd been freed from my facile intellect to become lost in an ocean of passion.

Still, I hadn't completely lost my mind. I asked Bobby to get tested, just to be sure.

"I'm not going for any tests," he said. "I had enough of that."

Oh, right. I thought. Because of the Accident.

But I couldn't quite stop being reasonable. "It would just be nice to know if I need to keep using something, or if I should go ahead and get this operation, or something ..." I started out.

He gave me a dark look. "I'm not trading my peace of mind for yours."

It was a puzzling expression, like a line from a Dylan song.

"OK," I thought: even if he's wrong, it wouldn't be so bad if I got pregnant. It wouldn't be the end of the world.

A few months later, when we were lying in bed, Bobby told me he'd been looking for someone like me. He loved me. He loved the kids. We came from the same kind of background. He wanted to get married. I wasn't sure what he meant by the same background — he'd grown up on Long Island, in a regular suburban Jewish family with a mother and a father living together. But that wasn't why I said no. For once in my life, I didn't want to get married. That was how much The School had changed me: I wanted to be free.

I don't know why I changed my mind again. I didn't just love Bobby, I was enthralled by him. We lay in bed between bouts of mad lovemaking, stoned, watching TV, and he would say he wished he had a Coca-Cola, and I would get up and get dressed and walk to the corner store and bring one back for him. It wasn't a purposeful wanting to make him happy — I moved in a trance. I'd like to think he hypnotized me into marrying him, but of course that wasn't true. I just changed my mind a couple of weeks later and told him yes.

Nora clapped her hands in satiric glee: "The children will have a father!"

"They already have a father," I reminded her. They spent every weekend with Peter. She gave me that silly grin, that I never knew what she meant by.

The night before our wedding, Nora gave us a special bachelor party. She fixed a plate of little treats and we all took acid and Quaaludes and she made love to both of us. The next day Bobby's friend John rented a big car and drove us all to Reno and we got married in the Washoe County courthouse. We were smoking pot all day. On the way home, Venus sparkled in the horns of a crescent moon. I thought it a wonderfully auspicious omen. A couple of weeks later Nora decided to move back East, and there we were. A family.

Bobby had his friends build a room for him in the attic, so he would have a place to write. He wrote every day; when he started working at the phone company he got up early and wrote before work, and more when he got home. He was ambitious about his writing, but aside from that he had not a care in the world. And what might have looked to other people like immaturity was to me a childlike charm. I was in love. Singing back-up to Bobby's lead, my romantic longings were all fulfilled. He was my rock-and-roll true love, singing those songs to me.

Nora was gone; our piles of money dribbled away and we got jobs and settled into a more regular-looking life. Leaning on his cane at the park, Bobby taught Josh to play catch. Nina sang along with us. We had dinners of macaroni or meatloaf; the children bickering and talking about school. We went to baseball games and rock concerts and the kids' school programs, where Bobby always sidled away during intermission to smoke a joint. He was not too wicked a stepfather, though sometimes his severity shocked me. When I tucked the children in at night I'd say, don't listen to what he says, you are good children. And they were good: if they suffered, they didn't show it. They had their own world, inhabited by a collection of stuffed animals with a walrus for president and a raccoon who owned a pizza parlor to provide employment. And Bobby and I had our imaginary world, too.

Oh, those nights! We swallowed Quaaludes and Percodan, sniffed coke, smoked more bud and went flying through the ethers. I'd told Nora that I couldn't see Bobby being the only person I would sleep with for the rest of my life. But that was my mind talking. My body had its own voice. While the children slept downstairs, Bobby and I became the people of our dreams. For hours we played parts in the stories we invented; we made an erotic theater complete with props and costumes. We gave each other new names, took on new identities. Schoolgirl and seducer, prisoner and guard. We played gin rummy for slave time. We put on each others' underwear and tied each other up. We transformed ourselves into fabulous creatures with no ties to earth except the flesh and juices of our bodies. The drugs brought me to a spectacular level of feeling, seemingly endless orgasms felt everywhere in my body.

There was another, more exotic element in our games: the psychic tricks I'd learned from Ray. I could make my mind blank, then press a fingertip to a small bone on a wrist or a cheekbone, then breathe and press until I could feel the pulse of my own blood through that fingertip. Then I'd find the deeper pulse in the bone and join them, close the circuit of the body's own inner ecstasy, the love of the heart for its blood, until the fire rose like spilling lava cooking us together. Bobby surrendered, relaxed. Once we were married he was sure of me, he had no need to strive. And it seemed the pain that had twisted his body also had its gift, its reversal into purest joy. For all the torment he'd experienced, he'd been paid some compensation. And I was spirited away from my everyday life: the care of house, cats, children. If during the day I was a busy Wendy, as soon as the sun fell I became another Lost Boy with Bobby. As our hearts beat in unison he held me above him to fly. I did not exist: bliss.

This is how we sailed through the air on our good ship Bed, writhing on the satin sheets, stopping only to inhale from the magic pipe of dreams or take another of the bootleg pharmaceuticals that made our brains dance. Downstairs my children slept, or perhaps lay awake whispering reassurance to each other, hearing our strange songs. We were gone: we had crossed into another dimension.

And every morning we crossed back. At daylight we separated from our shared scent and sweat. We showered, moving like woozy zombies into the day world, fueled by coffee and a morning toke at the bong. I helped the kids with breakfast and getting ready for school and dropped them off on my way to work. Buzzed all day from the joints I surreptitiously sucked on during breaks outside, I sat at my desk in a happy cocoon of dreams, because I was truly loved. I stared without seeing at the typewriter, the telephone, the files, the roomful of co-workers at their own metal desks, and remembered what it felt like to be adored. I was the luckiest of women, reveling in what others only fantasized about.

At day's end, I picked the children up at after-school care. I had dinner to fix and little questions to answer. As soon as Bobby came home he went to his attic aerie to smoke and write, faint strains of Springsteen drifting down through his trap door. I was often cranky and edgy. I could hardly wait to get to bed again. I didn't eat much. As soon as the dinner dishes were washed and the children tucked in, Bobby and I took our pills and began our night games: perfume and silks, lengths of soft rope, ice cubes in a glass beside the bed, spinning stories off each other like hobos around a burning trash can.

Bobby carried his pot everywhere the same way Peter had carried his Progressive Labor Party newspapers. I liked dope too, just as I'd liked Peter's politics. What I didn't share was the obsession — Bobby's need to use it all up, to keep going until it was gone and then send me out for more. I had always taken drugs when I was in the mood and put them down when I got bored or wanted to do something else. But now I was living in Bobby's country, a foreign land. Sometimes I wanted to go back home, but I loved him. And it gratified me to make him happy, like nursing a baby.

Bobby had a mean streak, a sharp way of speaking when he didn't like something we said or did. He was surrounded by barbed wire, booby trapped for the unsuspecting booby who offended him. He didn't hit or shout but he could say cruel things. Driving home once after a day at my mother's swimming pool, he proposed a scenario to Josh and Nina: "If your mother was the only one of us who could swim, and all three of us were drowning in the ocean, she'd save me first. She can always have more kids."

Oh, my babies! Their stunned little faces! What was he thinking, to say such a thing? That night when I kissed them goodnight in their beds, I told them Bobby was a liar and an asshole. Of course I'd save them first! But I couldn't say anything to his face. I had never liked fighting; I was terrified of conflict. Mostly, my feelings were well tamped down, and if I felt the beginning of resentment or anger, I'd meditate to calm and steel myself. I meant to talk to Bobby, I really did, I rehearsed what I would say, but as I waited for the right moment, as if he sensed it, he'd come home with a bouquet of flowers and give me a hundred dollar bill to buy coke. He'd make a magical altar of my body. And I ate it up, every bite. I cleaned my plate.

I had noticed before that there was a pattern of treachery in my life, but I still didn't see that I was my own betrayer. Once again I'd found a partner to collude with me in denying who I was. Bobby adored me — at least he adored somebody who had some similarity to me — and obviously, I liked the person he loved better than I liked myself.

Months stretched into years. I left one job and began another, the kids passed from grade to grade. Bobby finished a novel, his agent rejected it, he started another. He was getting a few gray hairs; I saw lines spreading from the corners of my eyes. I thought we would grow old like this, melting together night after night.

One summer weekend when the kids were with Peter, we went down to the central coast, near San Luis Obispo, to a house party for someone we knew from The School who had just moved there. It was an adventure; we didn't usually travel so far for a party. Bobby didn't like parties at all; usually, I went by myself and fielded questions about him: how come he's not here, what's he working on these days, is he doing The Work? Meaning the meditations and exercises of The School, which bored him. He told me I could do it for both of us and that way he'd get enlightened with me.

I could see a glimpse of beach beyond the dry hills. Our friend's new house had some land around it, and it was close enough to the ocean not to be too hot. We arrived in the afternoon and ate some barbecue. I had a couple of beers. I don't know why I felt so quiet and clingy; after all, these were my friends. Bobby played his guitar and sang, a small group gathered around him. I joined them, not quite sitting at his feet, but you could have looked at it that way. The sun was just setting. We were outside, in the country. It was a warm July evening, warmer than it would have been at home in San Francisco.

We slept in a small borrowed tent, wrapped in sleeping bags zipped together. In the middle of the night, we woke to a banging noise coming from a toolshed about a hundred yards away. Bobby poked me.

"Go see what that is."

I didn't want to leave the sleeping bag. The fog had come in; it was cold and damp now. I didn't know what the noise was — what if it was something dangerous?

That's what Bobby must have thought. Even in the dark I could see he looked afraid.

"Go on!"

I felt a flash of resentment. Why didn't he go himself? He was the man, the husband. Then I remembered: he was crippled. He had trouble walking. It was dark, the ground was uneven. He could fall.

I got up but I didn't look in the shed. Like a kid on a dare, I ran over and ran back.

"It's nothing," I said. "Go back to sleep."

I was starting to feel tired all the time. The doctor said it was stress, but he didn't have any suggestions for what to do about it. By then I'd lost my job in the recession, and my two or three part time jobs added up to more than one full time one, except they paid less. I had the two kids, in school now but still needing maintenance. I wasn't a single mother, but I wasn't sure how much of a help Bobby was. When he got home from work every day he went up to smoke pot and write until dinner was ready. Every day when I came home I rolled a joint for myself and set about with the kids doing all the things mothers do in the early evening. I thought being stoned made it different.

My mother noticed that I was fading. Later on that summer, she rented a cottage in Aptos, near the beach, and we all went there for a week. Bobby smoked pot and wrote, I smoked pot and took the kids to the ocean. We danced with the waves, looked for seals in the water and shells in the sand. At night we adults smoked and drank and played cards. It was a small cottage, and our other games were more restrained. And I was so tired all the time.

What made me start to count on my fingers that day? It was impossible. Once I had longed to have a child with dark curly hair and clear green eyes; a sweet singing voice and a way with words. But Bobby couldn't have children because of the Accident, or maybe it was because of all the x-rays. Doctors had told him he was sterile. We'd gone bare, making love night after night after night for over five years, and every month my blood came. Except this time.

I cried. I cried, and couldn't stop crying. The days when I had longed for Bobby's clever, musical child were distant. I could barely manage the life I had. Josh and Nina were getting more independent, I had a little space to breathe. Secretly, I had begun to write poems. But more than all that, I cried because I knew what those drug-filled nights meant. I was probably already in the ninth week of pregnancy, and I had been pumping toxins into my baby's blood all that time.

"What's wrong?" Bobby asked. "You could still have a baby. I mean, it's not like you're a ballerina or something."

I shook my head. "Are you crazy? With all the drugs I've been taking?"

Bobby sneered. He had a special contemptuous look when he thought something I said was exceptionally stupid.

"It's way too small to be hurt by that."

Now it was my turn to think him stupid. How could he be so ignorant? I shook my head and blew my nose. I couldn't speak.

I didn't want a baby, but even if I did, this one was much too risky. And Bobby would never understand that; in order to understand he would have to give up his certain belief that the drugs we stuffed ourselves with so greedily were harmless — innocent — and that wasn't going to happen.

I looked at him with my weeping eyes. "I just can't."

I cried! But this torrent was washing the scales from my eyes. It was the beginning of my return to sanity. Now I remembered the real world, the endless need of an infant, the months of half-sleep waiting on the edge for the summoning cry. Not much sex then, no more wild nights — but Bobby wouldn't know that. He lived in a parallel universe; in his mind we were just like any other normal family. Like his parents, having a late third child. And I was not quite ready to see that Bobby was a child himself, still less that that was what drew and held me to him so tightly: he was my own lost boy.

A week later I lay on a narrow table in a blue paper gown, knees raised and apart, my feet in the familiar metal stirrups. Bobby sat on a stool next to me, holding my hand. The doctor put an instrument inside me; I felt the pinch as it passed my cervix. The machine in the corner of the room began its hissing hum; Bobby squeezed my hand. I felt a sharp cramp and I started to cry again.

I knew I wasn't just losing my baby. I knew I was going to lose Bobby, too. I didn't quite know that I was sick and tired of getting high, that within a year I would turn away from dope completely, that I would also leave The School, that I would find the Sufis, that I would embark on great new adventures and regain more than I had ever lost. I cried. Even though neither Bobby nor I knew it yet, I had already turned away from him. The dream I had been living was already fraying around the edges, dissolving as I began to awaken.

'73 Datsun, Green: Runs Good

A lot happened in the fall of 1983: I ended a terrible marriage, and then my youngest sister died. And I was broke, I didn't have a job, and the terrible husband was taking the car with him. It was his car anyway; he'd only let me drive it when he felt like it. He let me use it to drive the kids back and forth to school. And one morning on the way to school just before he moved out, I cried: What was I going to do without a car? My sister hadn't died yet, that was something still floating like a black cloud in the unknown, waiting to happen. That morning I cried because I didn't know how I was going to get a car.

My daughter was religious at the time: "Why don't you ask God?"

Oh, she was right, I was the one always telling her to pray when I couldn't solve her problems, like get her more friends or understand math for her. I don't mean I ordered her to pray, it was just a suggestion I made out of my own desperation.

Like most things we tell our children, this one came back to me.

"You're right, Nina," I told her. "Good idea. I'll pray on it."

The next day I told her: "God told me to ask Grandpa."

Doubt nibbled at her faith. "*He* won't give you a car."

How did she know that? I knew my father loved me, but he wasn't a present-giving Daddy. He was a solid Daddy, never violent to his family, an advice-giving Daddy who sometimes surprised me with favors. He'd once put a new electrical circuit in my house — a hot, unpleasant job — and once he'd given me twenty dollars for my birthday. That was a while ago; maybe it had only been ten. I bought a bottle of Old Bushmills and toasted Daddy, happy-high. He was a fine Daddy, just not a big present-giver.

So now I told Nina: "God didn't tell me Grandpa would give me a car. He just told me to ask."

She didn't know what to say about that, and we'd arrived at the school. A kiss and a wave.

When I came home I called my father, shaking a little, scared to ask for such a big thing. He wasn't home. He was in Nicaragua helping people, making heart monitors out of discarded TV sets.

My stepmother was sympathetic but I was embarrassed. Actually, this was my third divorce, and I thought I should have known better. I knew it was my own fault I was in this situation.

"Oh, we'll help you," she said. "Don't worry, I'll ask him as soon as he comes back."

She didn't even mention what was wrong with me to marry such an asshole in the first place. She'd been smart: she'd married my dad. She didn't say anything like that.

But while my father was flying back from Nicaragua, his youngest daughter — my baby sister! — was in Cambridge, giving all her stuff away.

While he was home in Oakland, sleeping off jet lag, my sister was drilling holes in her exhaust manifold. My sister the engineer worked very carefully. She didn't want to screw up the job this time. This was my sister Nikki, beloved of my father and stepmother, cherished by me and Annie, especially adored and coddled by our other sister, Jody, my stepmother's daughter who my father had adopted. Worshiped by our baby brother. A girl with a brilliant mind and beautiful golden hair; a guitar player, a fixer of cars, a flyer of gliders.

The summer before her junior year in high school Nikki was something of a trial to her parents, and they had sent her to stay with me and Peter, to help us move to our new house. She made us a metal sculpture to hang on the front porch; she held baby Josh on her lap and read to him. I missed her when she went home and wrote to her sometimes, but she was young and busy and didn't return my letters. She went on to MIT and rarely came back to see us, or her parents.

And then, last summer — her last summer — Nikki had finally come to visit. She was sweet to her parents and took me and the kids up for glider rides. She even came with me to Joe Miller's walk in Golden Gate Park, a rag-tag band of seekers and screwballs. She'd stood at the edge of our dancing circle, wary as a deer. As we gently broke the circle and began our walk to the beach, she took off suddenly, with a feral lope, racing ahead of us on the path. She was waiting when we arrived at the beach, her long hair flying in the wind like a golden flag. She did not want to hear about joy or love. She had already decided she was through.

Jody called me from New York at six in the morning, passing on the grim news from the Cambridge police. I borrowed my husband's car and drove across the bridge praying, because it had fallen on me to tell our parents. I thought that was just about as bad as it could get, the pain filling their living room, exploding out the windows. A rumbling dusty stink bomb of anguish and grief.

My father bravely remarked that in Nicaragua, where he had just come from, tragedy was commonplace. Everyone there was so young because people didn't live long. And my stepmother, very strong, had seen her German town blasted and burned to ashes, practice for the bombing of Dresden. She never said much about that, but I'd looked it up. The firestorm sucked all the air out of the center of the town, suffocating the people in the underground shelters. The ones outside melted into the pavement. She and her family lived on the edge of town — they were spared, but eleven thousand people had died in a night. She had been, then, a few years younger than Nikki ever lived to be.

I wasn't thinking about the car.

But a few days later when I was visiting, my father mentioned that he'd heard I needed a car.

I screamed, "How can you talk about that now?"

But he could, and pretty quick it turned into an argument because I wanted an automatic and he said a stick. Much more practical, save your brakes. Better mileage.

"No," I said, "I live in the City, the hills — "

He described a device he'd heard about or perhaps invented that held the brake for you when you were stopped uphill — that way you'd have both feet free for the clutch and gas. It sounded nuts to me and I told him so. Then I felt bad because I didn't want to hurt his feelings. Nikki had only been dead for a week.

He said a stick shift was better all around.

What I didn't say was that I'd never learned to drive one. But going home on BART, I told myself I'd learn.

He told me he'd look around, and I looked, too, racing him to see who would find one first. My old friend Willy drove me to Fremont to look at a Toyota. For sale by Mohammad, an old guy in a white robe. I was glad Willy was there. He rode in the back while I drove with Mohammad sitting on the edge of the passenger seat. It was a nice little car — an automatic, of course.

But the steering felt a little weird, and then Willy asked Mohammad what that noise in the rear end was, and suddenly Mohammad's English wasn't so good.

On the way home Willy and I stopped at a park under the Dumbarton Bridge and talked about what Palo Alto used to be like, back when we first knew each other. My father and stepmother, with Jody and Nikki and our brother, had been living in Palo Alto then, too. Willy used to pick me up at their house sometimes when I was there for the weekend; he remembered the blond toddlers playing on the front lawn.

A couple of weeks later I'd looked at a lot more cars that weren't right. Then my father called: he found a nice little Datsun, a '73 with 80,000 miles. Four doors, he said, that would be convenient, with the kids.

He met me at the North Berkeley BART station and we drove to a graduate student housing project in Albany. The husband was at his lab; we talked to the wife. She had all the papers spread out on the table. There were some kids' toys on the floor; she was a little younger than me. She said they were from Israel.

We went out to the carport. It was a cute car, awfully green. First thing, I looked in through the window: Two pedals! An automatic after all! I loved it, I was so happy! My daddy was buying me this great car. I named it Esmeralda.

"Yes," I said. We went back inside to get the pink slip. My father gave the woman a check and told her about how a tree was planted in Israel for him even though he wasn't Jewish. It was because he'd been in the Spanish Civil War. We all shook hands. My father and I walked out together. He told me to go to the DMV office in El Cerrito because the lines would be shorter. I listened, grateful and superstitious. If he had told me to circumambulate the building seven times before going in, I would have done that, too.

That car was very good to me. In seven years, all it needed were tuneups, brakes, a set of tires. The mechanic told me it could go to 200,000 miles. Except sometimes it overheated, or seemed like it was going to. My son Josh learned to drive and borrowed it, and he said sometimes it wouldn't start; he thought the starter was going and I replaced that. Josh graduated and went to UCLA, and then I was afraid to drive it all that way to visit him, sure it would overheat or break down outside of Buttonwillow or some other timewarp desolation weirdness twenty miles from a phone.

Then, suddenly, my mother bought herself a new Honda and gave me her old one. For a month I tried to sell the Datsun with signs on bulletin boards and ads in free papers. People called and said they wanted to see it and I waited around, but they never showed. Willy told me to put an ad in the *Chronicle*.

I would have been happy to get five hundred for it, but he said you have to ask seven to get that. So my ad said: '73 Datsun, $700. Willy said, "Put that it runs good."

The first guy who called had a Spanish accent and came over when he said. He told me he was from Puerto Rico and had a job in the farmers' market. There's not too many people from Puerto Rico in San Francisco, but I used to know a lot of them when I lived in New York.

I asked him if he knew that game with the big jar of water and the pennies, where you drop a penny through a slot in the jar lid, trying to hit the shot glass in the bottom. The water deflects the coin, so it's harder than it looks. If you get your penny in the shot glass you win a quarter.

This guy hadn't heard of that game. I'd thought it was a Puerto Rican thing.

We went out to look at the car. He walked around it two or three times. He asked a couple of questions and I offered to open the hood.

"Why?" he shrugged. "I don't know anything about cars.

Does it run?"

"Yeah, it runs good" I said. "It probably needs brakes. Do you want to drive it?"

"No," he said. "That's OK. How much?"

"Seven hundred," I said.

"OK," he said. "I got to go to the bank. Can you take me?"

Wait. I wanted to say. It's really only five hundred. But that would have been dumb. It would have made him wonder if the car was worth anything at all.

I looked up his bank in the phone book to find the closest branch. I drove him to Stonestown, wondering which one of us was crazier. He was paying the asking price for a car he didn't know anything about, and I was riding in a car with a strange man who could have been a serial sex killer.

He told me his wife was visiting friends in Seattle and when she got back, he was going to surprise her with this car. Take her places on the weekend, go to the country.

I told him again the car needed brakes. And he might need to do something with the cooling system eventually. He just nodded.

I waited in the bank parking lot while he went in for the money. What if he didn't have any? What if he was in there robbing the bank, and came out waving a gun, yelling at me to drive away fast? I shuddered. Life was precious to me.

He came out of the bank smiling. He still wanted me to drive. Back at my house he counted out seven big bills. I signed over the pink slip and told him how to get it registered. I felt good that I wasn't sticking him with any unpaid parking tickets. He was OK.

A couple of months later I saw him driving down Mission Street. I was glad the car was still running good.

The Trauma of Birth

In the center of one of the photo montages you gave me is a picture of you and your mother. You are a baby, about a year old; your mother is smiling, you are smiling, your heads lean together: two blond heads. She is looking only at you and you at the camera, which I imagine is held by your father, who must also be smiling. Your mother is very beautiful. She has never given birth.

And here I am, in the house I have lived in since you were that baby, in the City that I love like an old friend. Through the living room window I see three boys in baggy pants bouncing a basketball on their way to the park across the street. There's the grinding metal screech as the streetcar turns the corner. It's summer, and a dry wind blows the dead leaves and trash in the driveway into a little funnel, whirling like remembered images.

I'd met Linda in The School, where we meditated and sat in circles of nine, retelling the traumas of our lives. From this, Linda and I knew that we shared a sad and shameful bond: we had been unwed mothers who had given up our babies for adoption. We had the same wound, a pregnancy shaded by grief and jealousy, anticipating someone else's blessed event. We were mothers who would not be mothers this time. And when we looked into each others' eyes, we saw the same anguish: *not-knowing*.

Linda got married, moved to Napa, had a baby. For a few years we hardly saw each other. Then one day she called to tell me she had paid a "finder" and found a teenaged boy in a Philadelphia suburb, not far from where she'd given birth to him. She had spoken to his adoptive father, then been called by the family's lawyer. She'd waited two more years for her son to turn eighteen, then flown to Philadelphia and rented a Mercedes. She didn't have to tell me why she needed a nice car. The adoption agencies made it a point to tell us birth mothers how much better off our babies would be with parents who would be better providers than we could ever hope to be. I kept the finder's name and phone number in the small desk drawer with other special things: my passport, a two-dollar bill my father gave me when I was a little girl, an old photo of Willy.

And meanwhile, your eighteenth birthday passed as all your birthdays passed for me. I looked out the window onto the street into a wider world and tried to guess your name. I wondered where you lived, if you looked like me. What you thought about me. If you were good at math, or sports, or drawing. If you were all right or in trouble. If you were alive.

When you turned twenty-one I wrote to the adoption agency. I told them I knew that the law had changed, given you the right to find out who I was. I gave my address and phone number; I said I would notify them if I moved. I wrote that I was not breaking the agreement I had signed — I would not try to contact you or your family. I only wanted the agency to tell you who and where I was, if you ever wanted to know.

You made an independent decision to relinquish your child, the social worker wrote back. *We are sorry that you continue to have unresolved feelings about your decision, and that you no longer live in the New York area, where we could provide you with further counseling.*

When I caught my breath again, I called the finder. It would cost $250. New York is easy, she said.

I paid the money up front, like a drug deal, and your birth certificate came in the mail a week later. Precious piece of paper, with its red seal! There was your name, the name I hadn't been able to imagine. A nice name. I said it out loud, over and over.

I studied the paper for clues and found your father's occupation. A profession, that was good. I drove to the library and looked in the national directory. His address was listed: San Rafael. I felt feverish, focused, hardly breathing. There they were, your parents, in the Marin County phone book! You were here, twenty miles away.

But I would not, could not call your parents. They could not possibly want to hear from me. And you were grown now, not likely still living with them. And I wanted to see you, but I was also afraid of what I might find. Afraid you would not like what you found in me. Either one of us could be any kind of nightmare.

For ten more years I rolled on the tide between fear and longing. I became a spy. I made scouting forays into your territory, drove by your parents' house. I called the nearest high school, pretending to be a prospective employer, and found out that you had graduated in the top third of your class. I found out that your mother was an orchid grower of some renown, and sent a chatty friend on the pretext of buying one. She returned with a beautiful plant and new intelligence: you had graduated from Berkeley, a philosophy major. I relished these nuggets, even while I cringed at the unsavory deceptions I stole them by.

You must be somewhere! I didn't want to bother your parents. I went back to the library to pore over phone books in cities where I imagined you might have gone: New York, Los Angeles, Washington. I don't know why I was so sure you were in a city; I had no idea you were in mine.

Some of my friends gently tried to discourage me. They thought it unwise to look for you. They had a different point of view, had friends who had adopted children, it would be an invasion of your privacy. Of your parents' privacy. Or they wanted to protect me: what if you were crazy, a drug addict, a thief—what would I be exposing myself to? Why not just move on?

Because I had already let you go once, I could not let you go again. And my life *was* moving on. Josh and Nina grew up, left home. I published a novel. My doctor ordered a lab test that came back positive. I was mortal, I might be carrying a slow time bomb in my blood, though no one could read the timer. And there was something I needed to tell you. There was something only I knew, that you needed to know.

I needed to tell you that you had not been a mistake. You were not an accident. You were a wanted child, only the times were crazy and things had gone badly, and I was young and stubborn. I wanted to tell you that you were free to see me again or not, as you chose, that I would not pursue you but that I would stay, remaining solid in a way that had seemed inconceivable to me when I was twenty-three. I would remain for you, whenever you wanted me.

That was the message I needed to give you. After that, who could know?

I began to form a plan: one last lie. I needed a young confederate, a person who might plausibly have gone to school with you. A person who did not know me very well, who wouldn't need to stay involved or make a claim. And one day a strange, stick-thin young woman, Odille, appeared at my workplace. She was hired suddenly, without application or interview. Our director claimed they had met in the elevator when Odille was on her way to an interview at another company in the building, and in the time it took the elevator to rise four floors the director had hired her. An improbable story, but it seemed destiny had dropped this person in my lap.

She was young — younger than you — but she was a mother herself, she would understand. She wrote poetry, some of it good. She became attached to me, I was someone she could show her writing to and she was grateful. She wanted to do something for me in return, and I asked her for a favor. I gave her your name, and your parents' phone number. Call, I said. Say you're an old college friend who's lost touch. Ask for his phone number.

"Then what?"

"Then I want you to call him and ask him if he wants to meet me. And if he doesn't, I want you to give him a message."

Odille called me as soon as she'd talked with your mother. She gave me the number. You were living in San Francisco! I trembled. I looked in a reverse phone directory and found your address. I found you!

You were living five blocks away from me, around the corner from the post office.

Suddenly I had to buy some stamps.

I stood across the street from your house, shaking and grinning. I wasn't crying. In your window was a poster for rent control. When I'd come back to California the summer after you were born, the Summer of Love, when I'd joined SDS at San Francisco State, when Peter and I had marched in the streets, I'd worked on a rent control initiative, too. I'd had a poster just like yours in my window.

That's the first thing I tell you, the first time we talk.

The first thing you say on the phone is "I don't want to be on Jerry Springer!" I tell you I don't either. I'm not like that. But how do you know what I'm like? I don't know what you're like, either. This is the hard part: we don't know if we will like each other.

You are coming over, we are going to meet now, and I'm

pacing in the living room, afraid to watch out the window for you. And I have another secret, a deeper unease: Once, during the years when I knew your name but not your face, one early morning as I lay in bed between sleeping and waking, I suddenly remembered — or perhaps imagined — something. That summer when Joe and I had been trying to make you, we were fighting all the time. In the middle of an argument one afternoon I bolted, ran down the stairs and out to the street, looking for comfort. I ran to Alonzo, most beloved of old lovers. I lay down with him on his dirty mattress while his girlfriend was at work. He smelled of coffee and drugs. His dark copper skin was silky smooth. Now, I couldn't quite remember or figure out if I'd already been pregnant. And it might have been a dream, something that never happened at all. But that morning, with the memory of his smell, the feel of his skin, I was shocked fully awake from that half-dreaming state. Had that been your beginning? Did your skin gradually darken in the first months of your life? Had your parents wanted a baby enough not to care about your color? Was this memory or fantasy? In a few minutes, when I see your face, I'll know.

When I open the door every doubt is gone. You are not Alonzo's son. You look exactly like Joe.

We hug, and the excitement between us fills my house with an explosion of light. It's too intense, we can't talk for long. I give you a copy of my novel, my poems. We make a date. We can't get the time back, but we have time now.

Everyone makes history; each of us tells ourself a story, assembling a universe from pieces of memory. And in the years I was waiting to meet you, I told myself a story about what happened:

Joe's best friend Sal came back from Vietnam and they moved into the apartment down the hall from where Paul and I lived, on East 8th Street. The queers who lived in that apartment before had painted all the moldings gold, and Joe and Sal thought it was funny and kept it that way. Sal started going out with a woman I knew who lived downstairs on the fourth floor. And I started sneaking away from Paul to hang out with Joe. It was my last year of college. I'd tell Paul that Joe was helping me with a paper, and slip down the hall. Paul was spending most evenings at the races anyway.

In late December there was an eclipse of the moon, and that night when Paul was at the track, Joe helped me pack everything into my going-to-college footlocker and a couple of suitcases. We ran out into the night. From a phone booth on Avenue C, I called my mother collect and told her I'd left Paul. "Do you have another boyfriend?" She asked in a friendly way, not angry or upset. When I told her about Joe, she approved. She told me it was better not to be alone. I tried to remember when she and my father had split up — was she already seeing Louis Borosov?

I didn't move in with Joe right away. I wanted my own place. We took a cab, with my luggage, to Alonzo's old apartment on Norfolk Street. Alonzo had been doing a lot of dope and he owed five months' rent. He was about to be evicted and he wasn't really living there anyway; he stayed at his girlfriend's. I talked to the rent collector with his black hat and long sidecurls. I paid the back rent and moved in. It was just one room and a kitchen with the bathtub in it. The rent was only $35 a month.

I was crazy in love with Joe. He was hip and funny. Good-looking, too, with wavy blond hair and dark blue eyes. He took me out dancing, at clubs when he could afford it, and at the Old Reliable, a bar on 3rd street, when he couldn't. He loved jazz and blues, he was a reader of poetry and plays. He was working at the arts branch of the library and about to start acting school.

In June, the same day as my college graduation, I went to court and got divorced. Joe and I went to California to visit my mother, and then we went to Mexico for a month. Some strange things happened on that trip, but that's a story for another time. When we came back to New York we stayed in a friend's dumpy first floor studio on the Bowery, stepping over sleeping drunks to get to the front door. The light of hobo fires burned all night through the kitchen window. And then we found our own place. I was twenty-one and Joe was twenty-six.

That's the beginning of the story I tell you, when we first begin to meet. We both talk a lot, and we have a lot to say to each other. You tell me about your family; how you were cherished and loved. You always knew you were adopted, specially chosen, like being Jewish. Your grandmother called you "Little Philosopher." You were angry when your parents moved from New Jersey to Marin when you were ten. You went to Hebrew School and had a bar mitzvah. You liked to ride your bike and skateboard. You worked hard in school, but you didn't fit in. You hated the suburbs — just like me! You didn't register for the draft when you turned eighteen. You went all the way through college with good grades — you say you did this for your parents — and then you fell apart for a few years. You took a lot of bad acid in Berkeley: your post-graduate work. You were homeless, squatting, living in another world in your head. And then your parents took you home, helped you, found you a good therapist. You tell me you're glad I didn't find you ten years ago, that now is the right time.

Across the street from City Hall is a park with plane trees and a fountain with a long reflecting pool that has been dry for years. So many homeless people were camping there. The lawns were littered with stinky blankets and plastic bags, trash cluttered the beds of annuals. Hippie-looking activists came with buckets of soup and boxes of sandwiches and signs: Food Not Bombs. I saw them when I went to the library or the farmer's market nearby. They looked a little familiar. I didn't know you were among them; I didn't yet know who you were. We had once looked a little like that — Peter and I, and our friends, fighting against the war, against racism, against landlords. We must have looked just as angry, just as righteous, though we hadn't thought of burning and piercing our anger into our skin.

And this is you!

I can tell you all about myself, but when I try to tell you about your father, I realize how little I know. We were together for about two years, when I was still young enough to think two years was a long time. What I know better than I know him is the idea I've had about him for thirty years.

What do I remember? He was from Erie, Pennsylvania, the third child of four in a working class Catholic family. An Irish mother; a German father. I can't remember which of his legs was shorter than the other, shorter because when he broke it playing football his parents took him to the Catholic hospital instead of to the good one that would have set it better. He was the first in his family to go to college; he had a master's degree in English from Penn State. He came to New York when his best friend signed up for Special Forces and went to Vietnam. He married a woman named Valerie, he taught English in an orthodox Jewish girls' school.

He wanted to be an actor; he auditioned at a prestigious school and got in. The classes were during the day, so he quit his library job and went to work on the docks at night. He came home in the very early morning, his jacket pockets filled with oranges, tangelos, grapefruit. Sometimes he woke me then to make love. He gave me his pay every week, keeping out a little pocket money. He liked to cook, especially breakfast. He was good-looking and sexy; he was sometimes very tender. He was at least a little vain.

He looked so much as you do now. Shorter hair, in the style of the times, but a few years later he would have grown it long, like yours: wavy, dark blond, vaguely girlish. His face looked a lot like yours; you have the same Irish nose. You tell me when you went to Hebrew School the other kids asked if you were really Jewish. Yes, I can tell you now, you are a real Jew, a born Jew, the son of a Jewish mother.

But Joe's wild wordy Irish genes — I can see that in you, too. You are always polite with me, and sweet. You have been brought up very well, I see that, but I can also imagine what you're like when you aren't polite. Generations and a middle-class family have refined you; yet I see your fist-swinging, bottle-chugging ancestors behind your eyes, no-good boyos out havin' fun.

And here's another strange thing: you tell me you took a lot of acid; we took a lot too. I never had a really bad trip, but Joe had many, and when you describe your own bad trips there are the same images, just like his: the skull split open, the fallen-off limbs, the fizzy lightning.

We begin meeting regularly for breakfast at a neighborhood diner, Hungry Joe's. In warm weather we sit at a table outside on the sidewalk. We're getting to know each other. You know a lot about the city, and we talk about politics. I am delighted; your views are enough like mine that we don't really fight, but different enough to be interesting. I tell you how my writing is going, you talk about your job as a caseworker with homeless people. You are ardent, defending the down-and-out; you spend hours on the phone to get someone a hotel room, a medical appointment, a bed in a drug-treatment program. I tell you that your passion for the underdog reminds me a little of my mother, and it turns out that a woman you work with knew her, talked about her.

You're taking a vacation, to Miami. There's a little story here: this was your grandmother's apartment, and when she died your mother and your aunt decided to keep it as a vacation place. And it's kept the way it was when your grandmother lived there, a family museum. I understand, I have a room in my house that my daughter calls the "Ancestor Room," with my grandfather's custom-made furniture and pictures of dead relatives. You're going to meet an old friend in Miami, a sometime girlfriend who's been living in Washington. You speak about her as if she were still your lover, but you push that away when I offer it: no, no. I wonder when you will fall in love.

When you come back two weeks later, you have something for me. A large gray envelope holding three sheets of photo montages, pictures of you and your family. Your little boy face is just what I always imagined: that straw-light hair. Here's a set of smiley baby pictures. Here are your young parents at the beach, your mother on your father's shoulders. Your grandmother, grinning between a pair of Israeli soldiers. You shrug: It meant a lot to her. I nod, I know. Here you are smiling again, with a dog larger than you are. Here you are at your bar mitzvah, in tallis and yarmulke.

This is the childhood you've had without me. You are and you are not my son. I am and I am not your mother. We are two philosophers, tiptoeing along this ambiguous edge. I think of all the children in the world who are not raised by the women who birthed them: babies rescued from orphanages and earthquakes in foreign places. Children raised by relatives in far countries while their mothers work here and send money home. The babies of the

Polish ghettos, flung over barbed wire fences to other, Christian, mothers. City orphans shipped west on trains to be farm laborers for foster families. A universe of separation.

These are pictures of the other side of my long-time heartache. You have a family, not much less or much more happy than any other. Imperfect like all families, yet also perfect — for you, as mine was perfect for me.

In a Tibetan Buddhist initiation ceremony, the Rinpoche sits on a raised chair. Several lamas stand on either side. The lamas chant, bells ring, the incense rises. We, the new initiates, walk up to the front in a line, wait, slowly cross the platform one by one, stopping before each lama. The Rinpoche cuts a few strands of hair from the crown of my head, another lama sprinkles me with saffron water, another ties a red string around my neck. And the last one hands me a folded paper from a stack on a low table: my dharma name. And later, when the ceremony is done, each of us opens our paper and reads the name, Tibetan letters, then a transliteration, then the English meaning. We show our names to our friends, who also have new dharma names, and each person's name suits them so well! It seems such a random thing, a paper from a pile on a table. Yet everyone gets the right name. Each is perfect.

And this is how I begin to see our lives.

The apartment Joe and I found was farther downtown than we'd lived before. It was on Willett Street on the corner of Grand, five flights up. We had a tiny corner view of the East River, once we cleaned the years of grime from the windows. The apartment was huge: six rooms, and the grand luxury of a bathtub in the bathroom instead of in the kitchen. We peeled layers of old linoleum from the floor and found newspapers from the 1940s and '50s. We cleaned and sanded and varnished and painted. Joe found nice used furniture and carried it up the stairs.

I tried working for the welfare department for a few months, then quit for a succession of part-time arty jobs. We were hip and happy, we went to the Lower East Side bars: Slugs, The Old Reliable. We listened to Zoot and Al over plates of spaghetti at the Half Note; we ate stuffed cabbage and liver and onions at the Ukrainian restaurant on Avenue A. We cooked for each other and cleaned up together. We were crazy in love.

Hurrying on the way to meet you at a café in the Mission, I pass the yoga center with its carefully tended front garden. The scent of mock orange and jasmine almost covers the urine odor from the sidewalk. I'm late. Usually I'm the one waiting for you, now I don't want you to think this is pay-back. We still don't know each other very well.

"The phone rang, I'm sorry," I say breathless. Your face is in shadow; I can't see if you're frowning. Because in part of my mind I still believe I've wronged you, I'm always half expecting you to be angry at me.

But you aren't angry. You tell me about a book a friend of yours just published. I promise to buy it, read it. We talk about culture. Across the table I try to sneak a look at your hands, to see if they look like mine. I want to see your feet. When I look at your face I don't see me, I see Joe. I didn't remember exactly how he looked until I saw your face.

You show me a pair of scented votive candles you've bought at an art store nearby. You offer me one and I choose the jasmine, intoxicating. Neither one of my children — my *other* children — would buy a scented candle, but you tell me how much you love these fragrant things. As I do. Again I'm stunned by the links between us — how could you be so much like me, who you never knew?

We say goodbye outside on the sidewalk with a hug, and I watch you walk away. Your carriage, your swinging walk, is just your father's — yet you have never seen each other. You've told me that Ed Sanders, who Joe knew well, is a favorite poet of yours; you've given me a tape you made of the Fugs, who we went to hear every Friday night the summer you were conceived. When you were floating inside my body, could that connecting cord that nourished you also carry the immaterial impressions of my life? There is a spirit animating you, of Joe and me being together, the times we lived in. A life that was already made for you before you were born — perhaps, as Christians believe, before the world was made.

It's as if we had left you an invisible trunk packed with who we were: the music we liked, our old clothes, books, papers — like the time capsule my high-school class buried to be dug up and examined a century later. I can almost see you standing in the middle of our kitchen on Willett Street, with the windows and doors trimmed in red paint, the floor stripped to the boards and varnished; in the bedroom with the carved oak furniture Joe bought at a second-hand store, the green and yellow Indian bedspread, the matching curtain. The living room curtains were velvet, turquoise and purple. I bought the fabric on Orchard Street, the man beckoned me into the back of the store and felt my breasts and gave me twenty per cent off. We had a cheap Oriental-type rug. I can see you in those rooms, though that building has been rubble for twenty-five years.

You are very sweet to me, but you are angry, too. It comes out when you talk about the world, or our city. Your life, even. Your mind is sharp, everything is meticulously, beautifully analyzed and your conclusion is always dark. Things are bad, and they won't get better. When I say yes, the world is hard, but there's goodness too, and God is good, you smile patiently, painfully, as if I were telling you about Santa Claus. And I let it go.

How had I gotten into such a pickle? Of course you want to know. I was undone by my fascination with complexity and sensation; I had no desire for peace. It was the summer of 1966 and the rancid smell of the Vietnam War hung over the city. We were breathing something frantic in the stifling air. Walking home from a friend's one night I saw a young Puerto Rican in an army uniform standing on a stoop. He looked sad, smoking, looking at the street without seeming to see anything. Was he coming or going from the Asian jungle? There was enough for him to be stonefaced about, either way.

We sat on the floor with our friends, drinking coffee as the gravelly voice of Dylan, the bang of the Stones, the harmonies and bended rhythms of the Beatles poured out of cheap speakers. And then everything got faster, delirious. We smoked more pot and started taking acid. We didn't go out to hear jazz any more; we went to hear the Fugs. And suddenly Joe's acting teacher told him he was finished training, there was nothing more for him to learn there.

He was anxious and angry. He told me he needed money for photos, clothes. He told me I needed new clothes too, I needed to look good with him. I borrowed money from my friends and gave most of it to him. I went to Orchard Street and bought a moire-printed nylon mini-dress, bright colored bell-bottom pants, a broad-brimmed hat. Joe had photos made — the picture I would give you soon after we met. We took more acid. And Joe said: Let's have a baby.

I was afraid, but I was excited too. I stopped taking the pills in the plastic circular box. I dropped the little box on the floor beside our bed with the big oak headboard, with the bedspread matching the curtains, the green and yellow Indian print. I felt like I did when I used to get high on dope with Alonzo and ride the Cyclone at Coney Island.

I thought I was pregnant right away, because I didn't get a period for a month. Joe was so excited! I went over to my best friend Leah's, around the corner on Grand Street. It was summer, it was hot and dark inside her apartment; she had the curtains drawn against the sun. Leah had a little daughter, Abby, a toddler. We sat on her couch and drank iced coffee. I showed her my chin: "Look, I'm getting pimples, is that because I'm pregnant?"

"Maybe you're getting your period," Leah said.

When I did, a few days later, Joe hit me. "How could you do this to me?" he shouted. "I told everybody! You make me look like a fool!"

I cried. We tried again.

And then it worked.

When I came out of the doctor's office, when I had just found out I was really pregnant, I called my mother from the first phone booth I saw, around the corner on Lexington Avenue. I was crying, because Joe and I were fighting so much. We'd had a big fight that morning. It was hard to hear my mother's voice over the noise of the buses roaring away from the stop, the taxis speeding by. She was telling me to come home.

Part of the reason Joe and I were fighting so much was that we were taking a lot of acid. I loved the exhilaration, the swirls of light in the air, the way the walls billowed and the music turned into colors. If fear rose up, I rode its wave the way I'd body-surfed in the Pacific when I was in high school. Sometimes it's fun to be scared. But Joe's trips were different: dark and terrible, his limbs shaking until they fell off, his skull split open, oozing. The worse his trips were, the more acid he took — someone must have been telling him that was what to do.

Joe had finished acting school; now it was time to go to auditions. Time to make it in New York. He must have been scared about that. Maybe he already knew what I wouldn't know for many years: how it feels when you are pushing forward to your biggest dreams, certain that someday you — you! will sparkle with glory, a star! And one day, ahead on the road — you try not to see it, but there it is: the wall of the real world, as it is. You try not to look as you hurtle toward it but there's no escape from the crash. That might have been what was happening with Joe, or it might have been something from his childhood. It could have been anything. I don't know, really, why he was so angry all that summer. He said it was all my fault, and I thought maybe it was.

And then, because he had grown up in that kind of family in Erie, where his father worked in the mill and came home and drank and knocked his wife and kids around, Joe started knocking me around. A slap here, a slap there. A shove against the wall. Sometimes a harder hit. And then came the sorries, tears, promises. I loved him so much, but I was getting frightened, too.

I didn't tell my mother about the acid, the hitting. I just told her I was pregnant, and she told me to come home. I didn't go back to Willett Street right away that afternoon. I sat on a mattress on the floor of Adrienne's first-floor flat on 9th street. Adrienne was an old friend of Joe's and Sal's. She was round and short and painted big, wild, abstract expressionist canvases. On acid once, she ate a tube of cadmium yellow light because she thought the color would come out of her fingers and she could paint that way, no brush. She was crazy but I liked her. She was older than me, I felt comforted by her.

I sat on her mattress and called airlines to get a flight to San Francisco. Adrienne brought out Tarot cards and spread them out for me. There was the card of Strength: a woman in a long white dress bent over a red lion, the sideways figure eight of infinity floating above her head. She holds the lion's jaws in her two hands. Joe's birthday was in August — Leo, the lion. The card had a message: I would be able to hold his jaws. He would not bite me.

My mother picked me up at the airport in her red convertible. She was still living in the house I'd grown up in, on the south side of Palo Alto. There were the old cats: Cindy, her black fur tinged with red now, sleeping in a spot of sun on the vinyl tiled floor. Butterscotch, turned from orange to a soft gold, lying under a hibiscus bush in the garden. My mother was nice to me. She took me to Kirk's for a hamburger.

The next morning she drove me to a friendly psychiatrist who would say that I was suicidal so that I could have a legal abortion in the hospital. The doctor was very kind; we talked for a while. He asked about my life, about Joe. I told him we were still together, we just had some problems. He asked if I wanted to have an abortion or if I wanted to have the baby. He said he would help me, but I had to decide for myself.

I sat on the cool vinyl tile floor of my old room in my mother's house, the house we moved to when I was in sixth grade, the house I left home from to go to New York to college, to marry Paul, to meet Joe. I held the black phone, sobbing, listening to Joe yell at me. "Don't you kill our baby." His voice rose louder. "I'll kill you," he said. "I'll find you and kill you if you do this thing. I want our baby."

But his threat wasn't the reason for what I decided. I was afraid of him, but not that afraid. Once when we were tripping he'd put his hands around my throat. He said I was the problem, the cause of his torment. He started to squeeze. He said he could kill me. "It's your fault!" He shouted. "You don't take care of me! You don't love me enough!" I looked in his eyes: "Joe, Joe, don't do it, if you kill me I won't be here any more, I'll be gone. Forever." The "forever" spread out like water, the way words could sound when you were tripping. He took his hands away. I knew he didn't really want to kill me.

And I didn't want to kill you, even though you were not yet you. Whatever you were, whatever Joe was going through, I still believed we could work it out, like the Beatles' song. We could be a happy family. We had a future, and I believed it would be together. All of us together.

My mother sighed, and drove me to the airport.

For your thirty-second birthday I take you out for sushi. You choose a more expensive place than I usually go to, but I've never before done anything for your birthday, except cry. And it's fun! It's really good sushi. I'm having a good time. I take a sip of your cold unfiltered sake, it's something special. They have dozens of kinds of sake here. You tell me about a girl you met in yoga class. You like her, you've been trying to call her, but it's frustrating. She doesn't return your calls right away. It seems to be hard to get together. "Keep trying," I smile.

A couple of weeks later there's an e-mail from you. You have made your conquest. But when I see you again it's clear that you have also been conquered. The next time we meet for breakfast she is there too, a beautiful olive-skinned young woman, bright and sweet. I keep staring at your face to see what's so different, as if you've shaved a beard or grown one. Then I see — it's not hair but happiness that's changed your face. When we talk there's none of your usual dark argument, your pessimistic growl.

In front of my house I tell you, right in front of her, how light and relaxed you're looking. You laugh and kiss her on the head, and she laughs, too. I can see you together for a long time, you could grow old together, there might be a child. And what about that trip around the world you've talked about making? You might go together, you might find what you need without leaving home.

But it doesn't work out.

"It's not happening," you say defiantly when I ask about her a few weeks later. And now I feel your despair, my own despair, my bad example. Now I see all the girls and boys who've broken your heart. You tell me you don't want a relationship, you only want to be in love. You look to me as if for confirmation, because I've lived alone for so long. I seem to be saying with my life that you don't need anyone, that alone is fine. I tell you how much I enjoy my own company, my independence. I don't tell you about my loneliness, or my fears. Like any mother, I want you to be happier than I am.

When I came back from my mother's I took a cab home from the airport, over the Triborough, all the way downtown to the East Side on the FDR, past the hospital where you would be born in a few months. There were a bunch of people I didn't know crashing in our apartment, Joe's new friends. They were hippies from California, long-haired and barefoot in gypsy clothes and feathers, jingling with little bells. The hems of their long dresses and the fringes on their shawls and blankets were filthy from trailing on the New York sidewalks. They said at home they liked to do acid and drive on the freeway. That was different — we were always so serious about tripping, cleaning up the apartment first, putting on the right music. Set and setting, like Leary and Alpert said. Joe and the hippies went out a lot to visit people the hippies knew. I went with them once or twice but they were all doing speed, so I went to see my own friends instead. Everyone was so excited that I was pregnant.

I was only home a week or two before I was on a plane again, to meet my father and stepmother and my little sister and brother in Montreal. They lived in Cuba and they'd earned a vacation and some hard currency, but there were reasons they couldn't come to the US.

They were happy I was having a baby. They didn't care if I was married or not; lots of their friends had children and weren't married. We should come to Cuba, where nobody cared about such things.

"You're going to be an uncle," my stepmother said to my little brother.

He poked his sister. "You'll be an aunt, and make holes in the ground!" He spoke English with an accent; he'd been only three when they moved to Cuba.

I took the kids for a walk in the park. We went to the zoo and I imagined taking you to a zoo someday, showing you bears and lions. I was having a good time with them but I felt uneasy. It was like something gnawing at me, I didn't know what. Maybe it was just heartburn.

My father and stepmother wanted me to come to Cuba. They didn't know Joe, but they were sure he would be happy there too. It would be a much better place for you to grow up. "The people have hope!" said my stepmother, with shining eyes. Their maid had just learned to read, at the age of sixty. They'd heard about the terrible things happening in the US. They'd heard of LSD, a drug that made young people crazy, made them jump out of windows. I said that wasn't really true, but they weren't listening. They already knew everything. I ate my lunch.

When I got back to New York the hippies were gone, but new people were crashing with us — Barry and Israel, young, bearded speed freaks, studying kabbalah with an old rabbi on East Broadway. Other people drifted in and out too. Joe still didn't have any kind of acting job and he was only shaping up at the docks one or two nights a week. He had another girlfriend, a woman he knew from acting school. He told me there was nothing for me to worry about; she was a lesbian who only liked men sometimes. I didn't care that much about the girlfriend. I still saw Alonzo once in a while. We didn't believe in monogamy.

I had been back from Montreal for a couple of weeks. One night the phone rang when Joe and I were in bed, just starting to make love. "Let it ring," I said, but he got up and talked to his other girlfriend for a long time. When he came back to bed I didn't feel like making love any more, and he got mad about that and hit me.

I thought about you, growing inside my body. You hadn't started to kick yet and my stomach was barely rounded, but I knew you were there. Joe was yelling and hitting me and suddenly I jumped out of bed and ran into the living room, crawled in Israel's sleeping bag with him. I was trembling. I said, "Please hold me," but we didn't say anything else. Israel put his arms around me, stiffly. I could tell he didn't want to. He was really into his kabbalah thing and he wasn't supposed to touch women. Joe stormed around the apartment for a while, yelling about what a bitch I was, always letting him down, what a bad mother I would be, I didn't know how to take care of anybody. But he didn't come in the room where I was huddling against Israel in his sleeping bag on the floor. After a while I heard the bar on the police lock move, the front door open and close.

I hadn't been crying, but I started when I heard Joe leave. Israel was holding me by then, very delicately, muttering about the sound of flesh hitting flesh. I don't know if Barry was awake. I got up and checked the locks, even though I'd heard them close. I felt afraid.

Joe must have come back sometime in the next days, and I must have told him to go away. He must have given me his keys, I must have given him his things, his clothes and books, or maybe I gave them to someone else to give to him. Some of my friends talked to him, people that were his friends too. I don't remember that, but I remember Barry and Israel drawing kabbalistic signs on the walls and over the doorway, to keep him away. Then they left, too.

When she sees you, Susan smiles her beautiful smile at you and says, "I thought you looked familiar." My heart jumps up, yes, you do, you do look like me! My first words when I saw you in the hospital nursery, through the glass: He looks like me!

We are at your favorite Thai restaurant. We like to go out to eat together. We've been here before, you pointed out the careful presentations, the delicate pattern of sauce on the plate. They have unusual dishes here. Susan insists on a curry called Evil Jungle Prince.

She is the first friend of mine you meet. We are proceeding very slowly in trying to know each other, and the other people we know will add layers, new details to our constructions. We need time to assimilate what we're learning, a little at a time.

Susan is Leah's older sister. I've known her even longer than I've known Leah. Susan's daughter was born just a year after you, when my wounds were still fresh and oozing. I visited the hospital; I brought a little dress. When I saw the baby at her breast I thought: where's my baby?

I don't think Susan knows this; there are still a few things she doesn't know about me. But she's wanted to meet you, and now she does. She talks to you, asks you questions. She's a brilliant interviewer: in a half hour she's learned as much about you as I have in half a year. I listen.

We talk and laugh. The tendrils we've grown are beginning to weave themselves together. We are becoming part of each other's lives. The food here is good. You look good. I feel good, being here with you and Susan.

I didn't know where Joe moved to. I heard from friends that he wanted to get back together, to talk to me, marry me. But I wouldn't even see him. That's how I was when I was younger: I couldn't face him. I just wanted him to disappear. I didn't want to live by myself, though, so Leah and her three-year-old daughter Abby moved in with me. They had been living around the corner, in a building owned by the same man, Arthur Brown. He was a decent landlord; he met with us in the Willett Street kitchen and let Leah out of her lease. He looked from her to me and back to her and shook his head. "You're a girl, she's a girl — you're living together?" We told him we were just friends.

Leah taught me how to make pot roast with sweet potatoes and turnips. I showed her how to bake a chuck roast in foil with a can of cream of mushroom and a package of dried onion soup. I taught her Joe's recipe for baked ham covered with cloves and canned pineapple slices and maraschino cherries, basted with ginger ale. Leah was going to City College and working part-time and I babysat Abby. We were making a little family.

The doctor was bald and wore a bow tie. He had delivered my friends' baby. They liked him; they laughed about his bow ties. They said he did natural childbirth; it was the best. Leah said so too. He had an office like all the good doctors in New York, on a side street in the East Eighties. It was below street level, like a fancy restaurant. There was a brass plaque beside the front door. Ring to enter.

The waiting room was filled with pregnant women in expensive dresses and good haircuts. The doctor was nice, but then, he thought I was married. When things changed, I had to tell him I wasn't. He seemed annoyed with me for changing my mind. For lying, either when I'd told him I was married, or now that I was telling him I wasn't. "Which is it?" he snapped. I didn't like him any more.

As I left his office he walked behind me. "Try to take off some of that weight," he said. "You're turning into a little tub." He patted my behind.

I went home and spread chopped herring salad and red horseradish on a matzo. That was what I ate all the time. I also liked little foil-wrapped triangles of French processed cheese called *La Vache Qui Rit*. I spread it on English muffins, topped it with a slice of tomato and a couple of anchovies, and grilled it in the toaster-oven. I was getting big as a cow, all right. And sometimes I even laughed.

I waited for you to be born. I didn't know whether you would be a boy or a girl. I imagined singing you to sleep, the way Leah sang to Abby. You would like the French cheese triangles too, like Abby did. I would cook farina for you, and take you to the playground. I'd fall in love again.

There was a luncheonette on Avenue A across from Tompkins Square Park that looked as if it hadn't changed since the fifties. There was nothing self-conscious or fashionable about it — the

Lower East Side wasn't fashionable then. It was just a poor people's neighborhood, and things didn't change very fast. This place served club sandwiches and chicken salad and egg creams. They had an ice cream fountain, and signs on the walls with old-fashioned balloony letters advertised the special treats of my childhood: black and white, banana split, hot fudge sundae deluxe (whipped cream and chopped nuts), root beer float. There was a counter with red vinyl-covered stools, but we always sat in a booth. We played our favorite Motown songs on the jukebox.

Abby was very cute and smart. Sometimes she whined or wouldn't do what we wanted, but mostly she was sweet and biddable. She wasn't being bratty that afternoon. It was early November, starting to get cold. A smelly New York haze hung over everything.

I was always watching Leah, trying to learn how to be a mother. Maybe we would keep living together, raise our kids together, if neither of us fell in love. Both of us had boyfriends, heard each other making love on the other side of the wall. I had been dating a guy named Gene who was in Cleveland now, studying to be a psychotherapist. He came to New York every couple of weeks to see his parents, and me.

Gene wanted to take care of me. He saw I was hurt, messed up, and he wanted to fix me. The last time he'd been in town he'd called his uncle, a social worker, looking for help for me. His uncle said I should give up my baby for adoption, but Gene told him I didn't want to. Sitting next to Gene on the couch, I could hear his uncle through the phone: "She's being very selfish," he shouted. Gene started to argue but then his uncle kept yelling, and Gene hung up. I was crying. I was keeping my baby! Who did this man think he was, to call me selfish? He didn't even know me! Gene was sorry; he hadn't expected that. He was only trying to help.

I didn't have any kind of clear plan. I thought after you were born I could get some kind of job — I had a college degree, after all — and get a babysitter and get on with our lives. I was dating other guys besides Gene. Pregnancy had made me very popular with men, but I hadn't met anyone I wanted to marry. I hadn't fallen in love.

Leah and Abby and I sat in the luncheonette. Abby was wriggling, sliding and squeaking back and forth on the vinyl bench. I was eating a three-scoop banana split with mint chip, butter pecan and rocky road. Leah was sharing a hot fudge sundae with Abby. Abby started making a fuss about something. Maybe she didn't like the chopped nuts, or she wanted another cherry or more whipped cream. Maybe she wanted her own dish. Maybe she spilled something and Leah yelled at her when she was cleaning it up.

What I remember is looking across the table and knowing suddenly and absolutely that I wasn't going to keep you after all. I didn't want a baby. I was going to give you up for adoption.

Right up to that ice cream moment I had just gone on assuming that you were my baby, that I would keep you with me. But between one bite of butter pecan and the next, something shifted in me, the way you shifted inside my belly. You stretched out a foot, or a fist, and my mind stretched out to consider possibilities I had not wanted to look at.

I don't remember that I had any particular reason, or formed any kind of theory about my life or yours. I must have talked to people, made phone calls. Maybe it was the doctor, with his bow tie and his frown, who gave me the names and numbers, asked the questions. I told him I wasn't sure any more about natural childbirth, since I wasn't going to keep you. He was nice again. "You want the stuff that makes you forget everything," he said kindly. Yes, that was just what I wanted. Something to make me forget everything.

We don't plan it as a coming-out party, but it feels a little like that when you come to Thanksgiving with my friends down the coast in El Granada. I don't really expect you to take me up on the invitation, but you do; your mother doesn't cook Thanksgiving dinner since you and your sister left home. So when Margaret calls in October to ask who I'm bringing, I tell her I'm bringing you, and she hesitates only a moment before she asks me if I would like her to tell people who you are ahead of time, so we don't have to explain so much.

"Yes," I say. "Yes, please do." Margaret and her husband Tony are among my oldest friends, and for over twenty years I've been coming to the Thanksgiving party they host together with two other couples. I brought Josh and Nina when they were still living at home, and they still come sometimes, when they visit. For a few years when he was between wives, Peter used to come — he'd been friends with Tony since the sixties, when they met in the radical teachers' caucus. I brought my mother for the last few years of her life. She liked it very much, especially, she said, because it wasn't just family. She was too European to cook Thanksgiving herself; we had always gone to friends' houses when I was growing up. So this is the right place for us, too: we can be family, and yet not family.

We drive down early for the softball game before dinner. My cauliflower and cheese dish is in a box in the trunk. It's a beautiful road along the coast, the curves winding over the cliffs above the beach, then the flat green artichoke fields, the golden hills behind them. My home country. At the schoolyard that looks out over the ocean we watch and play a little ball. It's an easy, relaxed game — batters get as many strikes as they need until they hit the ball.

When the game breaks up, we get into cars for the short drive to the house where we will feast, the house made of old wood and light that Larry and Penny built almost by themselves. I give Scott and his grandson a ride, and you ride in the back seat with Scott. He is a giver, a Quaker, one of the kindest people I have ever met. He asks you about your life, questions that have nothing to do with me or with our weird relationship that we are still trying to figure out. I stop being nervous.

In the big upstairs room at Larry and Penny's, long tables are laid, with white candles in Aunt Jemima syrup bottles and the exquisite flower arrangements Emmy makes every year. People begin to arrive from the softball game, from their kitchens and televisions. This year there are about forty at our party — some long-time regulars, some here for the first time. These are my friends, and they are very proud of me this year because my novel has just come out. Scott has brought six copies for me to sign. Margaret and Tony's son Forrest has brought a few of his friends; one of them has been crewing on a Tall Ship that's in the Pillar Point Harbor now. After dinner we'll walk there for a private tour. Everyone is welcome here: ex-spouses and difficult parents, estranged siblings, problem children. All together. There are no judgments or arguments in this demilitarized zone — this is the neutral country of the heart.

Just before dinner, you and I are crowded with a little crush of other people in the kitchen, doing the dance of the casseroles, taking turns moving dishes in and out of the oven and the microwave. And suddenly, here's sweet, spacey Lucy, effusive and light. She shrieks as she meets you: "Oh! How wonderful! You've found your real mom!" I wince with you; you've told me how it makes you feel when people say: your *real* mother. As if your mother was a fake, an artificial mother, and I, who only grew your body in mine and then sent you away to your life, am somehow *real*.

When I introduce you I say your name, and sometimes that's all. How can I say it? My *other* son. My son-that-I-gave-up-for-adoption. My un-son. My son. You have a fine sense of language; you are precise with words. Like me, like Josh and Nina, like my father. And you have had a championship education in critical theory, you know how to unfold words and uncover their secrets. "I understand," you tell me. "I can say, you're my birth-mother, but you can't really say I'm your birth-son."

But I've begun to learn to listen to the question behind the question, the heart behind the words, and I see how, again, I've disenfranchised you. You *are* my son. I abandoned you; you were born in the middle of a hurricane and swept out of my arms. I built a reed boat for you, like Moses' mother; I would have sent spies to watch you, too, stolen into your parents' house as a servant or a thief, but I believed you were no longer my son, and it's the betrayal in that belief that shames me now.

We take our places at one of the several tables in this high-ceilinged room with its wall of windows. It's mid-afternoon — every year, we eat later than we plan to — and dusk is already beginning to reveal itself in the sky. Scott's mother is in a wheelchair, and three of the young men carry her in her chair up the stairs. The buffet is set on a long table against the wall. Here's a ham and a turkey, with gravy and Margaret's oyster dressing. Tony's made paella. Scott's baked several loaves of bread. And the rest of us have brought stuffings, vegetables, relishes, salads, treats. Cakes and cobblers and pies. Tony makes the sweet potato pie that his grandmother used to bring. His grandmother, and then his mother, used to give the blessing: Our Heavenly Father. They are both gone now.

Now Forrest offers the blessing, a meditation carrying us through the universe and back to earth. We are reminded to love each being, from the stars and the stones, through the plants and animals, to our friends, ourselves. When we go around the tables and each say what we are thankful for, I am thankful for you, that you are here, at Thanksgiving, and in my life.

The haze was so heavy over the city that week that we were all coughing. Abby's little barks woke us in the night, and then I'd hear Leah's own deeper cough as she got up for the Cheracol. My mother sent me a check to buy maternity clothes. Gene stopped calling me; I think I had too many problems even for him. Leah told me I was invited to Thanksgiving dinner at her aunt's.

It was a subway ride I'd never taken, to Queens. We came up from the station into that gray-burnt orange sky into a street of low red-brick buildings. It was unfamiliar, almost alien. I was far from home, for so long that the ache of exile and despair had come to rest, buried under an assumed identity. I had tried to make myself a part of this world of subways and soot, kosher delis and winter clothes. I didn't realize how far I was from my own nature. Like this city, I was covered in a haze.

At Leah's aunt's apartment, we squeezed into the small dining room, sitting too close together around the table: Leah's parents, her younger sister and brother, two aunts, an uncle, cousins. I wore a discreet smock: I had begun to show. You had begun to show. To make your presence known. When one of the aunts asked where my husband was, I said he was away. They could assume he was in Vietnam, in the war. Though the aunts complained that the turkey Leah's mother brought was dry, I thought it was a good dinner. I couldn't remember the last time I'd been to a family Thanksgiving. The year before, Joe and I had just moved into Willett Street and I'd made *canard à l'orange* from a French cookbook. Leah's family had a teasing, slightly mean way of conversation, and while I didn't feel unwelcome, I didn't feel like part of it, either.

I had hoped the aunts and uncles would think I had a soldier husband, but Leah's mother must have told them the truth — how could she not? They would all have talked, after Uncle Harold had driven us to the subway station and we had started on that long ride back to the Lower East Side, Abby falling asleep against me. A few days later I answered the phone, and Leah's Aunt Beatrice told me she knew some wonderful people who wanted my baby.

My stomach clenched and turned. This wasn't what I wanted. What wasn't what I wanted? I didn't know. I didn't know that what I really didn't want was for anyone else to have you. I stammered something that meant no. I hung up. Who were these wonderful people who couldn't get a baby from an adoption agency? Did I want you to grow up in that bantering, anguished world? Leah's mother sang all the time, she had been a professional singer before she married, but none of them seemed happy.

But I had already decided not to keep you. I couldn't change my mind. I didn't want to revisit that decision, to examine the feelings beneath that choice. I wasn't sure what they were, and I didn't want to think about it. I didn't want to uncover the pain I had hidden from myself. I called the adoption agency the doctor had told me about, the Jewish one. I wanted everything to be right, as right as it could be, anyway.

When we met, you were working with homeless people. Every one of your clients' problems captured you completely. You told me their stories of capricious bad luck and egregious mistreatment. Almost every night you stayed late in the office, interviewing, making calls. You are fierce with me when I suggest detachment. "Let go a little," I say. *"I have to care,"* you tell me. So I'm the one who lets it go.

Then at breakfast one Sunday at Hungry Joe's, over your banana pancakes you complain: you can't keep on doing what you're doing. You don't know what to do with your life. I think about the way your mind takes things apart, the careful way you use words, how you love to argue. I ask, "Why don't you go to law school?"

You shake your head furiously: "No, I don't want to do that."

" OK," I say. "You'll find something."

A few months later you have a new girlfriend. She's beautiful and wild — and ambitious. You are very much in love with her, ardent and protective. And you're restless. You surprise me one day, and tell me you're applying to law school.

Through the weeks of applications, the months of waiting before you are accepted, the beginning of school, your anxiety bristles around you like a spiky halo.

"Why are these transitions so hard for me?" you ask.

I think I know but I can't say it: that transitions are all partings and loss, and all partings resonate with that first awful parting, especially for you and me, they are all imprinted with the memory of our separation: the trauma of birth.

You are introspective, you have peered into the abyss, but I don't know if you have seen how badly you need to know who you are. That self will be there, ready when you are ready to go back to it, because he was right, my grandfather, your great-grandfather: birth is a wound we spend our lives trying to heal.

I don't remember the time between the ice cream parlor and the social worker's overheated office. It must have been December or even January; I was wearing winter clothes. The office was a tiny cubicle. The Venetian blinds on the window were yellowed. The social worker was older than me, but still young, in her thirties. She had neat dark hair; she was wearing a nice suit, Bonwit Teller.

The child welfare laws in New York then said a baby must be adopted by a family of the same religion as the birth mother. There were only three choices: Catholic, Protestant or Jewish, each with its own agency. "None" was not an option. I decided I really was Jewish in some deep down way that had nothing to do with chicken soup or Hebrew prayers, even though I had only been to a synagogue once, for a wedding. "Jewish," I'd told the doctor with the bow tie, and he had sent me here, to the Jewish agency.

"But not religious," I explained to the social worker. She was taking notes.

She nodded. "Reform?" she asked.

For a minute I misunderstood her. I didn't realize she was still talking about religion. I thought she was asking me if I wanted to change my ways. In eighth grade my friends and I were always going to "reform." Be a better person, we meant. Stop gossiping, stop swearing, stop chasing boys.

All the Jews I'd ever known were Reform, except for a girl I'd met in college who nearly starved because she couldn't eat the food in the dorms. I nodded.

"How did you happen to become pregnant?" was the next question.

I stared at her. I hadn't swallowed a watermelon seed.

She meant, the whole story. I don't know what she thought when I told her that Joe and I had wanted a baby, that I'd gotten pregnant on purpose. That *he* wanted a baby; I hadn't tricked him. We were both happy about it, being pregnant. I couldn't explain to her how things had gone so terribly wrong. I didn't know myself.

When she asked, I told her I didn't want to go to a home for unwed mothers. That's not what she called it; there was some other name. But I wasn't a teenager who had to be hurried out of town. I had a nice apartment and a roommate.

"Does your roommate know you're pregnant?" the social worker asked.

Another astonishing question. Leah was my best friend. She knew everything; it was her old apartment I'd always run to when I was still living with Joe. First with my happy news, and then later, in tears, when things got bad between us. When he hit.

The social worker's pen moved over the forms as I answered more questions. *How much education do you have? Your parents? Artistic ability in your family? Musical talent? Athletic? Any medical problems? And the baby's father? What was his education? What does he look like? How tall is he? His coloring?* She wanted to make a match. I fidgeted in the chair. *We have all kinds of good families waiting for babies. A family where the parents work in the arts, then?* She smiled at me, encouragingly. I nodded. Yes, artists.

I had boarded the train now, and it was picking up speed. It didn't occur to me to disembark; the journey seemed as inexorable as the physical process of your growing inside me. You were growing and I was growing, and we were growing apart. It did not occur to me to disembark; I don't remember that I wanted to. I thought the train was taking me where I wanted to go, and you to a better place than I would ever find.

Even though housing is scarce in the City in the middle of the dot-com boom, I'm having trouble finding a tenant for my spare room.

"I could rent your room," you say.

That scares me; it's too much intimacy. But he's your son! I berate myself for holding back. But I don't know you! What would happen if we started fighting? At close range, you could decide you don't like me much after all. You don't like landlords. I don't like the idea of taking money from you. The whole thing is too complicated. It seems like a bad idea.

And you're ambivalent, too. You like where you live now, in a flat with three roommates — a good friend and his girlfriend and another woman. It's not as if you were homeless. You just thought — it could be really neat, living together.

It does sound neat, but I'm too cautious, and in the end, I say no. I rent the room to a woman who turns out to be a pathological liar with an explosive temper, and two months later at breakfast I tell you what a terrible mistake I've made. I should have rented the room to you. But you're in a stable situation now. You don't want to move. School has started. Everything is working for you.

For another month I stew and fret about the crazy woman in my house, how to get her out. And then history happens. In New York, terrorists crash two airplanes into the World Trade Center. We are all more aware of mortality, uncertainty. People can go to work one morning and not come home. My son Josh and his girlfriend Cameron decide it's time to move back to California. Even though I know they're going to stay at Peter's big house in Oakland until they find their own place, I tell the crazy woman that my son is coming back and I need her room for him.

And then, God won't let me lie. Suddenly, the house you live in is sold. You're being evicted, you and your housemates are splitting up. You need a room, and I leap. "Yes." I tell you, "Yes. It would be great if you came to live here, in my house."

The week before you move in I'm in a panic. I worry that it won't happen. You'll change your mind. I dread answering the phone or picking up a message, afraid I will hear your hesitant apology. Afraid you will say no, I don't think it will work, after all. I found another place.

On the eve of the day you've told me you'll move in, I leave you a message. False cheer elevates my voice: "Hi! I still have a few things to move out of the room but I think we can do it together — I'll be home all day tomorrow."

When I get back from dinner there's a message from you. You are moving in! There's no mistake. I feel a mixture of happiness and horror that reminds me a little of dating. It's familiar: the risk of getting closer to someone. The fear of rejection that runs so deeply in us, in *us*, for good reason. I have loved you since before you were born, before you existed, loved you with all my heart. A mother's heart. And at the same time, I'm afraid of you. Afraid you can't really forgive me.

When we met I could see between us an ocean of longing and grief. We've both learned to sail very well on that sea; we have learned to find love where it is. We are loved and cherished by our families: your parents, my children. The connection between us has always existed in another dimension, running beneath that ocean of yearning like a cable carrying pulses of light. Whenever our eyes meet, the ocean dissolves. Still, I remember the feeling of loss as if I had a shelf full of souvenirs from that beach. I don't know what you keep on your shelf.

It was New York winter now, with the loveliness of snowflakes, the treacherous icy sidewalks, the dirty slush. Abby's nose was always running. Leah's cough got worse. I felt you growing and moving inside my body. I was waiting for you, but it was like waiting for someone at a bus station who's only passing through.

Except for my growing belly, I could have been like any other New York girl in her twenties. I wasn't lonely. Men Leah and I knew were always coming over; sometimes they even took us out. I was surprised that they still thought I was cute when I was pregnant, but I liked the attention. There was no one special; I didn't fall in love.

Leah and I cooked together and listened to Joan Baez, Dave Van Ronk, Mississippi John Hurt. Leah played the guitar and sometimes we sang together, sad old ballads. *Cold blows the wind o'er my true love ...* We didn't want to think about what was coming in the spring: your birth, our separation. My mother sent me Dylan's *Blonde on Blonde*. The music was changing as it moved from London to San Francisco; there were new bands with funny names. Buffalo Springfield, Jefferson Airplane. My sometime boyfriend Bill Moore, a poet I'd met in college, brought over *Surrealistic Pillow* and the first Country Joe and the Fish album. And he told me someone named Jerry Garcia had a band called The Grateful Dead. "Hey!" I said. "I know Jerry Garcia!" Now he was making records, and I was making you.

One summer evening in San Francisco I'm sitting in my big kitchen, watching the shadows fall over the garden. The ocean wind is coming in hard over the hill, pushing the fog in, flinging the fig tree and the huge *Belle Portugaise* rose into a wild boogie dance. I'm on the phone with my old friend Danny Amos. He's been despondent since his divorce a year or two ago. He tells me his visits with his son are too painful, he can't do it any more. He thinks he should stop visiting, give up, not see him any more.

"Don't do that," I say. "You have to keep seeing him. He needs you, and you really need him. Don't give him up," I say. I don't say: You'll regret it for the rest of your life.

Danny had come to visit me on Willett Street, from some other city he'd moved to after college. He'd never been to this apartment; he pointed around the corner to where his grandparents lived; they went to shul on the next block. We drank coffee at the round oak dining table that was always piled with papers, in the room off the kitchen we used as a living room. Through the window you could see a little piece of the river if you craned your neck.

Leah came in to say hello. She knew Danny from when he used to date her sister Susan. She was taking Abby to her parents' house on Long Island for the weekend. Danny asked after them.

When they'd gone, Danny asked me how I was, really, and I told him not so good. I said I was going to give you up for adoption. He looked at my stomach where you were sleeping inside and he didn't say anything.

We finished our coffee and put our coats on and went out; we walked down Houston to the IND station. We weren't talking, it was too cold. We went down the stairs into the subway, me walking carefully, waddling. We were taking different trains. I was going uptown on the AA, to my psychiatrist, and Danny was taking the D train to Flatbush, to his parents. We were saying goodbye, going in different directions.

On the platform, Danny said: "Don't do it. Don't give up your baby. You'll regret it for the rest of your life."

"Shut up," I said. I don't know if I started to cry. I didn't talk to him again for over two years.

But now we're talking, and I'm telling him he must not give up his son. He doesn't tell me to shut up. He's quiet. I think he might be crying

Sometime in February I wrote to my father. I told him I had decided it would be better for everybody if I gave you away to a mother and father who could take care of you. I tried to explain that I was a different person than he thought I was. I had been living in a different world, and it was hard to describe that world, those times, to him. We were in the middle of different revolutions. When I'd seen them In Montreal, he and my stepmother were appalled and frightened by what they'd heard about young people in the US, that was why they wanted me to move to Cuba. They had never heard the music I listened to. They thought any person who would take a drug that made you feel crazy belonged in a mental hospital. There was too much to explain in one letter, and we had never talked very easily anyway.

I sat in the Willett Street kitchen looking out the window, talking to my father on the phone. My stepmother was on an extension. It was a rare thing, to be talking on the phone with them; it could take days just to put a call through. This might have been the first time he initiated one. They begged me, if I would not come myself, at least to send you to them, to Cuba, where you would have a better life. And then? I wondered. Would I come to get you in a few years, when you already spoke a different language? Wouldn't it hurt you more to be uprooted then? Wouldn't you be confused about who you were? They might have thought that with you as hostage, I would join them in building their new world. But it wasn't what I wanted. I told them about the adoption agency. My father said it was barbaric.

As in other things, he was partly right.

And now, you are completely right — it's neat living together! I watch you washing up your dishes and see our likeness in the slope of your shoulders. We're both too busy to hang out very much, but the comings and goings, the casual heys and seeyalaters, your music drifting from underneath your door — all the little intimacies of cohabitation feel natural, easy. It's like living with one of my kids, I think. And then I remember: I *am* living with one of my kids.

One evening I find my way to your school. Your trial class is having moot court, and you've asked me and your lover to be mock jurors. It's been quite a while since I've been in a classroom like this: beige wall, fluorescent lights, desks and tables. My eyes find your beautiful lover and I sit next to her in a double bank of chairs with the rest of the mock jury. The others seem very young, chatting in groups, and I remember that you are ten years older than most of your classmates. But even the professor, who dons a judge's black robe for the exercise, is younger than I am.

The case — alleged sex discrimination in a mythical law firm — is presented. You will make the closing argument for the plaintiff. Other students make opening statements, call witnesses, examine and cross-examine. Your lover and I roll eyes at each other: we've already decided your team — the plaintiff — has won. You are the best.

At the break, over pizza, after he sees me talking to you, your professor greets me and asks how I know you. It sounds so innocent and natural; he can't realize what an impossible question it is. I don't know what you've said to him. I don't know how much you want people to know.

But I'm not on the witness stand, not sworn to tell the truth, the whole truth, and nothing but. And so I tell part of the truth, with a smile: "Oh, I've known him since before he was born."

The professor smiles back. "A friend of the family, then?"

In a manner of speaking. I make an equivocal gesture, perhaps a nod, and take a bite of pizza.

The professor glances over at you, where you're talking to your lover. He leans close to me and tells me what a good student you are. How bright. I agree, yes, you've always been very smart.

"It's more than that," he says. "He has a gift."

And later, when you stand and make your argument, I see what he means. As you move and speak and argue, I'm mesmerized. You are very, very good at this. And I know who's given you this gift, this power to command an audience with speech and movement. I see Joe, years ago, rehearsing Richard II, limping around our living room: *Now is the winter of our discontent ...*

Sometimes your lover comes home with you. She's dazzling and scary, like a brush fire, and I'm afraid she will break your heart. She is wild, like I used to be, fierce with passion and despair. You tell me about her crazy family, how she passed out at dinner, how her room is a shambles of tossed clothes and piled-up papers that drives you nuts. You tell me how she turns this way and that, she doesn't stay with anything. I say it sounds like she lets everyone else tell her how she is.

"She needs a center," I tell you. "When she finds her center in herself, she'll be less susceptible." I remind you that I said the same of you a year ago. "Remember?" I ask.

Your face closes in a pained smile.

I say, "You're getting more centered now. She just needs to know herself a little better."

But she won't get centered, she won't get to know herself, she'll spin faster and farther and knock you tumbling with an especially cruel and ill-timed betrayal, the day before your finals start. You grit your teeth through your tears, we hold each other. You tell me how stressed you are. And you've anticipated this, warned me, or maybe yourself. For your whole life you've responded to every change and challenge this way, as if going into battle. You can't quite believe you're good enough, that you will succeed. I nod. I'm still like that too.

When you have a few days off between exams I tell you, tentatively, afraid of your reaction, that the next door neighbors are starting a big construction project on the other side of your wall and outside your window. I'm worried about the noise, the dust. You tell me then that you've been trying to reach the friend you were going to look for a place with last summer. That if he isn't interested you'll get your own place.

You are moving out. I am slammed. You've pulled a doll's string in me, and the mechanical voice inside repeats the words on the contract I signed so many years ago: ...*finding that I am unable to provide a home for my child* ... Slowly I realize that we have reenacted a drama, a précis, during these months you've lived with me. I count on my fingers. Nine months.

You are very kind; you phrase it all in terms of your own needs, not my deficiencies. You are right, you have needs that can't be met here. And I have needs too. I'm worried about finding a new tenant. I've gotten used to you. I won't like anyone else as much. And maybe I won't find anyone at all! I'm worried about the rent, I'm worried about money. And there's a deeper anxiety, my fear that I am inadequate to the task of my life. The same fear that you have, that leaves you sleepless and tense.

And suddenly I understand something. You are terrified of failing: at your exams, at school, at your life. Yet from my point of view I can see you are brilliant and hard-working, that failure is inconceivable. I know that you will do well in your exams, that you will excel at school. That you will graduate with honors, that you will have a brilliant and successful career. That you will make your parents very proud of you.

And though I can't quite yet feel it, I know that just as I see you, there is One who sees me, who has the same confidence in me that I have in you. Who loves me as much, or more — seventy times more than a mother loves her child, says the Q'uran. Who knows me completely and has faith in my abilities. Who has confidence that everything is all right for me, as I have confidence that it is for you.

Yes, you need your own place. You want to put bookshelves up in your living room. You want to buy your own furniture. You want your own kitchen, to cook with your own pots. You can't live in a room in someone else's house forever.

Our hearts are constructed with a cover composed of our every past experience. My past experience — my disgrace and sorrow at being unable to provide a home for you, my child — suddenly rises. Painful as that is, now there's something sweet about this, a vindication and a completion. It's satisfying: you are grown. You want your own place, your own ant invasions, power outages, broken sinks.

I dream that you tell me you are graduating, and that you want me to be there, with your parents. I say, all right. When I wake up I feel peaceful, at ease with what is. You are grown up, it's time for you to leave home again. We are not done with each other, it's only one chapter coming to an end.

Bill Moore didn't take me out on dates but he brought little presents: records, flowers, even a Smithfield ham from a trip home to Virginia. He loved me, but I didn't want to marry him. I didn't want to change my plans. When I talked to my psychiatrist about him, she didn't seem to think that marrying Bill was what I needed either. When she asked why I was still seeing him I didn't have an answer.

I saw Dr. K. every Friday afternoon at her apartment on Central Park West. She was an old Viennese lady, very kind, someone my grandmother knew. Her apartment reminded me of my grandmother's house: dark European furniture, Oriental rugs, the smell of furniture polish, a maid to open the door. No one was paying her to see me. It was a professional courtesy, a favor to my grandmother, who was now demented and in a nursing home. My mother told me that Marilyn Monroe had been a patient of Dr. K.'s and left her a million dollars.

My mother had also found me a part-time job at a small academic library. It was boring work and didn't pay much, but it was something to do. The head of the library was an old friend of my mother's; that's how I got the job. I was a girl in trouble who needed help. I wore a wedding ring, a thin band Leah had given me for Christmas, when I started to show. It was so I would look respectable, when I went out into the world.

I hardly ever talked to the other people at work. There were only a few, and they were all older than me. One day one of the women asked me if I wanted a boy or a girl. "Either one," I said. Another woman laughed and said, "Oh, she doesn't care. She'll keep it, either way." No, I thought. I won't keep it. Either way. The next day, I quit the job.

The City bought our building to tear it down for a new expressway. The children played "the building is falling down" in the halls and the downstairs lobby, home-made play therapy. Around us everything was rocking and rolling and we hung on to each other, Leah and I; we hung on tight to Abby, and to you, still swimming inside me. Our happy home was about to fly apart. The sense of looming catastrophe was palpable, whether in Saigon, or Jerusalem, or right here on Willett Street.

Before that first afternoon you came to my house in San Francisco, a grown man, I only saw you once. You were behind glass, like visiting someone in prison. You were three days old; I was standing with my psychiatrist, looking through the nursery window. The nurse held you up; you cried. Dr. K. held my hand. She stood straight and strong, she couldn't save Marilyn Monroe but she would save me, she will make me see. She told the nurse to fold back the blanket, so that I could see your whole body, see you whole and perfect. She was a doctor, the nurse did what she said. You were crying in a red, twisted face, but still I saw you, and I said in pain and wonder: "He looks like me!" The nurse wrapped you back up in your blue blanket. The card on the crib said *Baby Boy Veltfort*.

"He looks like me." I couldn't really tell if you did or not, but it seemed like something I should say. It was true enough about something that I felt: that you were part of me, a part that was being torn away.

I did not see you being born; I was unconscious. I had come to the hospital cheerfully with a magazine and a radio but two or three hours later I was splitting with pain. I asked for drugs. What they gave me did nothing for the agony, feeling you would rip me open as you struggled to get out, to become your own self. Instead of stopping the pain, whatever they gave me made me hysterical. I shouted and sang until the exasperated doctor knocked me out with gas. When I woke up, he was wiping his hands. "You have a baby boy," he said. But I didn't really have you.

"You had a baby boy." A West Indian voice, like a soft, pungent breeze through palm trees.

There was a young woman in a blue uniform reading the chart at the foot of my bed. I was sore and dazed. It was the morning after you were born; I was in a hospital room with three other women. It was not a maternity ward, they'd spared me from having to look at happy husbands bearing bouquets, nurses bringing tiny blanketed bundles to be breastfed.

I had a dull headache. The nurse's aide was pretty, the color of whole wheat toast. "Yes," I said.

"Where is your baby then?" Curious, not challenging.

I told her you would be going home with another mother. A mother and father.

"Ahnd why is that so?"

I shrugged and tried to explain that I couldn't keep you.

The aide shook her head. "You will miss your baby," she said softly. Definitely.

I only saw you once, behind glass, like visiting someone in prison. But which of us would be doing time?

One afternoon just before you move out, you come into my room where I'm watching a ball game. You ask me what my favorite color is and I know you're going to give me something. I tell you I like all the colors, I don't have a favorite, and you say, just pick one, and I say, "OK. Blue."

We haven't been getting along so well since you found your new place. You're eager for the landlord to finish getting it ready for you so you can move. You're making your own home, shopping for furniture and kitchen things. This morning I told you, truthfully, that I'm happy for you. You asked me if I was upset and I said, no, not upset, and you jumped in, the way you do, and said, "I know you're sad." Sad, yes. I'm sad. And also stewing with the brokenness of something, finding fault with you: you are self-centered, you don't think of me. And here you are, thinking of me. You've brought me a present.

You hand me a small chapbook with a blue cover. Five poems, your poems. You run out of the room, saying I can tell you about them later. But when someone hands you poetry, the world has to stop. If poetry can't stop the world, what use is it? So I turn off the baseball game and reconcile myself to being a few minutes late for my dinner date, and I read your poems. They are very good; they are interesting. Even the one about your lover's betrayal, still too red and bloody to be as good as the others, has a wonderful image of her, secretly planning the breakup as if she were building a ship in a bottle.

There is something else I see here, in the very first poem. Later that night, when I get back from dinner, I look through a metal box in the far back corner of my closet for a home-made magazine that Bill Moore put together with a typewriter and mimeograph machine the summer before you were born. *The Catfish Review.* Joe has two poems here; and this poem of yours reminds me of them. Lying in bed later I wonder if he is still alive. I've offered to help you find him but you're not interested. I suppose I'm enough for you to handle.

Soon after you move, you invite me for dinner at your new apartment. You cook an impressively elegant meal: fresh scallops, a good steak, lovely sauces. I bring a bottle of wine and a small gift. You are easy to buy music for. I've brought you a CD of Gyorgi Ligeti, a composer my mother liked very much too. You promise to make me a copy.

You've often given me copies of your music, CDs you package in jewel cases with your own home-made labels, wonderful collage. Like things I used to make, years ago. You tell me you'll make copies of all the music I've given you and I'm surprised you remember my gifts. I'm surprised, again, by your tenderness behind the irony and harshness. Again, you remind me of me, when I was younger. It hurts to remember how I was. I need you to find some peace, some love for the world as it is.

But this story isn't just about me and you. You are the Missing Child, the *Ur*-heartbreak. Don't worry — I don't mean *you,* the man sitting across from me as we eat fresh cantaloupe ice cream and talk about work and love. Not you, the man who worries about passing exams and getting a job, or me, once again looking for someone to rent my room, anxious about money, hoping to sell my next book, wondering if I will ever fall in love again, or if you will. Not us, personally — I mean the essence of our connection, the wires on which our story is strung. I don't know what I mean. I try to reach across all that to know you for who you are. I reach across the table with my eyes to your face.

When I dreamed that you invited me to come to your graduation, I thought it was a metaphor. But no: now it's happening. You are graduating from law school and you call to tell me you want me to come. I'm going to meet your parents. I can't tell you how much I don't want to do this. I'm terrified. But this is something you want, maybe something you need, and I will do it.

At the last minute, your sister can't come and you have two extra tickets. I can bring Josh and Cameron with me. I'm relieved, I'll have people from my tribe. Why do I feel so threatened, so fearful of being scrutinized? I feel the shame of our history, of my own resentment and jealousy of these people I don't even know, who've done nothing to hurt me, people who only wanted a child. People who love you, good parents. People who were good enough to have my son, when I was not.

And the day arrives. I dress carefully in my black Eileen Fisher dress. Black is best. I add a patterned black and white silk jacket that Susan gave me, for elegance. I try on scarves but they are all too busy with the jacket. And then I remember the white silk one in the shelf under my altar table.

Your graduation is at the Masonic Auditorium at the top of Nob Hill, around the corner from the Theosophical Society Lodge where for ten years I went two or three times a week to be with my friends, my teachers, Joe and Guin Miller. The white silk scarf was

Guin's, a legacy. Now I pray to their shades: Help me do this, I ask Joe. Help me find a parking place. Don't let my car break down. Don't let me break down. Don't let me be an embarrassment, the crazy birth mother. The one who still can't let go.

Josh and Cameron ride with me, and here's a perfect parking place only a block away. As we walk up the hill. I wrap Guin's scarf more closely around my neck, smelling the old couple's wise love in a soft residue of sandalwood. I feel them walking on either side of me, Joe lopsided from his once-broken hip, Guin with her beautiful posture. For some perverse reason, I'm wearing a half-slip that's too long and has to be rolled up at the waist. The elastic is loose and I can feel the slip starting to slide down over my hips. I'll be hiking it up all afternoon. It's as if there is a demon in me, bent on making me look like a poor relation. *You're a good girl,* Guin used to whisper in my ear when she hugged me. I hear her whisper now.

There's a huge crowd. I don't see you. I don't know what your parents look like; I couldn't look for them even if I wanted to. Cameron squeezes into a seat. She's hugely pregnant, only five weeks from delivering my first grandchild. We're early, waiting in these uncomfortable seats. Josh is bored. We read the list of graduates' names in the program, counting. How many Matthews, Jasons, Davids. Noahs. Two Winstons. A Bradley. We only look at boys' names, because we know the baby will be a boy. Cameron and Josh haven't decided a name yet. And there's your name! You are Magna cum Laude! You didn't tell me. Even though I don't deserve any credit for you, I'm proud: my brainy Jewish genes.

The program begins, predictably dull. A graduating student makes a funny speech, a judge makes a serious one. Over four hundred names are called, one by one. We cheer for you, and I listen and look for other cheers for you, trying to see where your parents are. The clock is ticking. And then the ceremony is over.

The three of us go downstairs to the basement, where we've agreed to meet you near the refreshments. Long folding tables hold vats of sweet, red punch and platters of dry sandwiches. It's a jostly, exuberant crowd and we move around clots of happy families, trying to stay out of other people's photos. Finally you find us, I hug you, you tell us to wait while you get your parents. I ask Josh to bring me some water. And here they are. Your pretty, blond mother, your tall, slim father. You.

Your mother and I look at each other.

"We did good," she smiles at me. She is short and a little plump; she reminds me of Susan. She could be someone in Susan's family. Her clear blue eyes look directly into mine: We did good. "Yes," I whisper. "Thank you."

I don't say: I'm sorry to barge into your life. Sorry I sent my friends to stalk you, to spy on you, to lie to you. Sorry to disturb your peace, your pride in your son.

It's crowded and close here, and your father suggests we go outside. On the steps, your mother says to me, "Just so you know, the Wise Agency is no more."

I don't like the reminder. I don't want to reminisce about this. I'm tongue-tied; I smile.

"Things change," I manage. It seems strange that she and I share such animosity for the organization that brought us together. But not so strange: they wrote me a mean, patronizing letter. They said they wouldn't help you contact me, even if you asked. You've told me they refused to help your parents find a sibling for you. Your sister was adopted privately, through a lawyer.

Now that we're all standing together, I see how much you look like your parents: For all its faults, the agency made a good match. Your mother and father are smart and artistic and secular, just what I wanted for you. You are so obviously what they wanted:

their son, handsome and healthy and bright. How could anyone not be grateful for you? Even with the problems you've had, the troubles you've caused them: the stripes of parenthood.

But I don't want to talk about the adoption, and I don't want to ask your mother what you were like when you were a baby. I don't want to cry. As we walk to the park across the street, I fall in with your father. He says it's so strange, that I was living so close to you, all that time. I explain how I came from here, this is home to me, and I came home after you were born. And you, I accuse him, silently: You always wanted to live in California. I didn't follow you, I didn't hunt you down. But we don't talk about destiny. We talk about baseball.

It's Mothers' Day and songs about mothers are playing on the radio. On this station, it's songs about mothers whose sons are at war and I say a prayer of gratitude that neither you nor Josh had to go, or wanted to. One of the first things you told me was that you never even registered for the draft. Amazing! And Josh, in the car from the airport when he came home from UCLA the night of the first Baghdad bombing: "If they call me up I can't go, I would refuse an order to kill." I cry for the mothers of soldier sons and daughters, and the mothers who are themselves at war now. The mothers whose houses are bombed and bulldozed, whose kids are blown up by land mines and not-so-smart bombs, incinerated with napalm and white phosphorous. All those mothers who grieve for children who they will never be reunited with.

You'll take me out to dinner tomorrow; today is the day for your mom. I cry for her too — her disappointments, her determination. You were already three months old when you came to her; she didn't know you. She started from scratch to build her motherhood, loving not a jot less, without that deep, physical connection that comes from growing, from blood and mystery, a new human being inside your body. I'm glad she got to be a mom. And I say it again, at my kitchen table: *I'm glad your mom got to be a mom.*

You take me to a very nice restaurant where I've wanted to go for months. It's trendy and too noisy for my old lady friends, but the food is spectacular. You are already there when I arrive and I worry that I am late but no, you tell me, you were early. The waiter pours from a bottle of champagne. You brought it, you came early to have it chilled. A special surprise.

And we have the usual good talk over our good food: your work at the law office, my writing, city politics. You have a new girlfriend, but one with an expiration date: she's expecting a job in another state and she'll be gone in a few months. You don't want more, and you do want more. It's an old story for you; an even older one for me. After dinner we walk to my car. I drop you at your apartment on my way home. It was a wonderful evening. And I'm sad.

A few days later, I'm driving home from a movie, remembering my mother and how movies were her cure for every unwelcome mood. She was right, my head and heart are cleared. I feel light as air, driving up and down the hills toward home, a sheer fog fallen over the city, delicate as a butterfly's wing. The scent of jasmine rises from the scarf around my neck. I think of my love for this city, and my mother's, and yours, and I'm amazed all over again that we were drawn to be together here by that inexorable gravity that moves in the world to bring together those with work to do with each other. I see that I've known you, not only for all your life, but for all of mine. There are templates of spirit that we are made to fit ourselves into, steps in our lives that we have already danced.

Those years when we did not know each other were not empty, they were filled with all the things everyone fills their years with. We hardly speak now about our lack even to ourselves. Your two birth certificates lay nestled together blindly in their envelope in the Hall of Records, as our separate lives were veiled from each other, as if there was always another me, another you, and those two others were never apart. We can see them now like shadows, dancing.

Photo by Nicho Mageras

Ruhama Veltfort's poetry and fiction have appeared in *Whispering Campaign, The Antrim Review, The Noe Valley Voice, Sound Journal,* and *Moonfish.* She is the author of two poetry chapbooks, *Whispers of a Dreamer* (Hollow Reed Press, 1983) and *Miles on the Bridge* (Wordrunner Chapbooks, 1997), and a novel, *The Promised Land* (Milkweed Editions, 1998). A new collection of her poems, *Translation of Light,* is forthcoming at www.echapbooks.com. She lives in San Francisco, California.

LaVergne, TN USA
15 December 2010
208918LV00005B/154/P